First Responder Families:
Caring for the Hidden Heroes

By
Tania Glenn, PsyD, LCSW, CCTP

No part of this publication may be reproduced, stored in a retrieval system, or transmitted in any form or by any means, electronic, mechanical, photocopying, recording, or otherwise, without the written permission of the publisher.

Text Copyright © 2020 Tania Glenn
All rights reserved.

Published 2020 by
Progressive Rising Phoenix Press, LLC
www.progressiverisingphoenix.com

ISBN: 978-1-950560-25-7

*

Printed in the U.S.A.

Editor: Jody Amato

Book cover design by Kalpart.
Visit www.kalpart.com

Book interior design by William Speir
Visit: http://www.williamspeir.com

Praise for *First Responder Families: Caring for the Hidden Heroes*

"Although first responders are often hailed as heroes, the unsung heroes are undoubtedly the families. As rewarding as our profession is, it comes with a price both physically and mentally. Tania's book is a much-needed insight into what a first responder family needs to know about the ripple effect of having a loved one serving their community."

James and Becky Geering

"This book is spot-on. As a law enforcement family, we underestimated the impact a trauma could have on the officer. We **severely underestimated** the impact it could have on family and loved ones. This book is a must-read for every first responder relationship and department."

David and Jennifer Mohr

"One of the most overlooked parts of a first responder's career and the things they experience during their career is the effect on the family. *First Responder Families: Caring for the Hidden Heroes* is a great read. Using real-life stories and experiences, this book offers solutions, inspiration, and hope for first responder families. We have been a first responder family for thirty-four years. We survived, but we went through some very dark times just not knowing how to handle and cope with some of the issues that are specific to our family. This is a book we will be recommending to others."

Chris and Cheryl Fields

From the beginning, *First Responder Families* drew both of us in. I've read your other books and attended your training sessions several times. Dawn has listened to me talk about your work and the passion that I feel to help with your mission in my little corner of the world.

When I read your book, *First Responder Resilience*, I remember saying, "She wrote a book about me. This is crazy!" When we read *First Responder Families*, my significant other kept saying, "I feel like she's talking to me." Your books are just that good!

I want to give this book to every new employee who walks in the door. I want to leave it in the lockers of all of my coworkers right now. I want their husbands, wives, partners, parents, and significant others to read it.

You have a gift, Tania. Thanks for sharing it with us. I pray the rest of the first responder world gets hold of this book soon.

Melissa and Dawn

Front Cover Photographs:
Author Photo: "Tania Glenn and Tyra" by Jill Hays, (www.jillhaysphotography.com). Used by permission of the photographer, © Copyright 2020 Jill Hays.

"Paper people cut outs representing union," Stock Photo ID: 446080by KTSDesign, used under license from Bigstock.com.

Back Cover Photograph: "House in flames," Stock Photo ID: 197755705 by asafaric, used under license from Bigstock.com.

Illustrations:
"Diagram of Maslow's Hierarchy of Needs"
© 2006 J. Finkelstein. Used by permission
https://commons.wikimedia.org/wiki/Commons:GNU_Free_Documentation_License,_version_1.2.

Author Photograph: "Tania Glenn" by Jill Hays, (www.jillhaysphotography.com). Used by permission of the photographer, © Copyright 2019 Jill Hays.

For the families.

Table of Contents

Introduction i

The Story Behind the Documentary iii

Chapter One: This Work Changes Families 1

Chapter Two: Managing the Negative 20

Chapter Three: Vicarious Trauma 38

Chapter Four: Traumatic Events and Families 65

Chapter Five: Public Safety and Children 80

Chapter Six: Pure Public Safety Couples 94

Chapter Seven: The Unthinkable 106

About the Author 122

Introduction

We all have that moment. For me, it's the sound of the garage door going up. If I don't hear the door, it's our dog alerting that the door is going up. This is the moment I breathe a sigh of relief. Another shift is over. Another safe return home of my beloved officer. Another shift closer to retirement.

We all have that moment. For some, it's the sound of the key turning the lock in the door. For others, it's the sound of the door alarm chiming. And for some, it's the stomping of boots on the front porch. Whatever it is—this is the moment we pray for, hold our breath for, and are thankful for when it happens.

No one understands this moment better than we do. As public safety family members, we live through it all—the worries, the unanswered text messages, the panic we feel when a story breaks on the news, the unanswered follow-up text messages, and the state of fear we all enter until we hear from our loved ones.

Being a family member, loved one, significant other, partner—whatever you are to your public safety professional—is an experience that is hard to define. In this book, I speak to the families and loved ones of public safety personnel—law enforcement, fire, EMS, communications, corrections, and flight attendants—not only as a professional with over twenty-eight years of experience working with first responders and their loved ones, but also from the heart as a family member myself.

We are all in this together. My goal is to provide you with inspiration, hope, solutions, and wisdom. And if you need help, please reach out.

The Story Behind the Documentary
First Responder Resilience: Smashing the Stigma

Having worked with public safety for over twenty-eight years, I have seen a sharp increase in awareness of trauma and stress in the law enforcement, fire, EMS, corrections, and communications communities in the last decade. There is now much more awareness and many war stories told, but there is little dialogue about answers and solutions. While it can be helpful to a degree to share a story of trauma, without any options or answers, it simply leaves the entire community of public safety asking, "So what do we do?"

I decided to create a documentary to offer hope, solutions, answers, ideas, and options. I wanted to highlight the stories of seven amazing people who walked through hell and came back. None of them were disciplined for getting help. None of them lost their jobs. All of them healed and are still on the line.

In this documentary, viewers are able to hear the stories of what happened to the cast, as well as what we did to mitigate the stress and heal the trauma. Every cast member took the steps to heal. They trusted the process, committed to healing, did their homework, addressed setbacks, and ultimately conquered their traumas.

First Responder Resilience: Smashing the Stigma was produced by Jacob McCloud from NOVVA Agency. It was funded by the Texas Municipal Police Association. It can be viewed anytime at:

<u>www.smashingthestigma.com</u>.

Chapter One

This Work Changes Families

If you cried out for more
If you reached out for me
I would run into the storm
Just to keep you here with me
I have gone beyond my years
I've wasted half my life
Did I save you?
'Cause I know you saved me too

"Song #3" by Stone Sour

Welcome to the world of public safety! Over time, this job changes everyone involved. It is inevitable. Everyone adjusts in some way to the culture and lifestyle of emergency services. For some, it changes them a little. For others, it changes them a lot. And for a few, it changes their lives forever in ways they never would have imagined.

Working in emergency services is not an eight-to-five job where one turns work on at the beginning of the day and turns it off on the drive home. Because of the nature of the work, it just isn't that simple. While working in the field of public safety is a career with set shifts filled with distinct responsibilities, it is much more than a "normal" job. From the first class or academy a public safety person enters, the transformation begins. This work becomes a way of thinking and living. It can and will impact every facet of life.

The moment family members of first responders realize that their loved one is changing, the family transformation begins as well. Families soon realize they are adjusting their lifestyles around the nuances of public safety work. This change also is inevitable. What matters most is how family members go about this transformation.

In my work, I have noticed three types of familial adjustments to the careers of first responders, based on the family system's introduction to the public safety world. Families are either Divers, Adapters, or Veterans.

Divers

People who "dive in" to the public safety world are typically those who meet and begin a courtship with an emergency services person. They are essentially drinking from a firehose to learn the nuances of the public safety lifestyle. They are quickly introduced to the public safety schedule of rotating shifts, day shifts, swing shifts, night shifts, twenty-four-hour shifts, forty-eight-hour shifts—you name it, welcome to the world of first responders. Divers quickly begin to understand that date night is not necessarily Saturday night, that weekends might be Monday and Tuesday, that cereal for breakfast might be at 4:00 in the afternoon and that nothing is quite normal in the world of public safety.

Divers also simultaneously begin to comprehend the type of work that public safety personnel do. They hear some stories and learn very quickly that their compass of what they consider awful is nowhere near what first responders consider awful. Divers are challenged to adjust this compass over time as they are progressively exposed to their loved one's stories from work. They begin to navigate the world of public safety into their psyche so they can integrate this world into their own. Over time, Divers who pursue long-term relationships with their public safety loved one typically become more desensitized to the stories, as what they consider awful merges into alignment with their first responder.

The other facet that Divers must adjust quickly to is their first responder's sense of humor. Generally, by the second date, Divers realize that first responders use humor as a coping mechanism. Divers who realize this are able to adjust to the sense of humor and even adopt it over time. Initially a person who begins to date a first responder might find the humor crass or inappropriate. The more a Diver understands that the humor is not meant to be disrespectful, and the more they understand that the humor is used to offset the awful, disgusting, or horrible nature of the things first responders are exposed to, the more accepting a Diver can become of public safety humor.

Divers also soon learn that being with a public safety person involves a completely different mindset. Because first responders see and deal with the worst things that happen to people and the worst days of people's lives, first responders tend to create their worlds around them in a way to try to avoid such events happening to them. First responders frequently avoid events with large crowds. They sit with their backs to the walls in restaurants so they can see the doors. First responders can be very distrustful of others and often avoid meeting new people or starting conversations with strangers. They trust fewer and fewer people over time and rarely expose themselves to situations where they feel vulnerable.

All of this is a significant shift that Divers have to take on. The key is understanding why first responders think and feel the way they do. One of the issues we hear in family therapy is how upset a first responder gets when their loved ones forget to text them when they arrive at a location or when they get home safely. When we ask a public safety person to explain to their loved one what they envision when they don't get that "I'm home" text, their response is typically that they go to the worst-case scenario and their loved one is "dead in a ditch." This usually helps a Diver understand why these new communication patterns are in place. First responders fear the worst for their loved ones based on what they have seen and experienced. When someone is running late or is unreachable, their thoughts automatically turn to the worst-case scenario because of what they have experienced.

Tips for Divers

Adjusting to a relationship with someone in emergency services can be both fun and a bit intimidating. One of the best things that couples can do is communicate a lot about the nuances of a public safety career and how it feels to adjust to it. Divers should also consider attending any sort of events for family members that they can. If a department is hosting a family day or some sort of social event, it is very helpful for Divers to experience this. Meeting other loved ones, watching how public safety personnel interact, learning about the job, the equipment, what first responders do to maintain safety—these are all important things for Divers to experience.

Another way for a Diver to begin to truly understand their emergency services loved one is to ride along with either their public safety person or someone in their department. This is a unique experience that teaches so much about taking calls, boredom followed by bouts of chaos, adrenaline spikes and dumps, shift work, fatigue, and the many other issues first responders face on a daily basis. I have found that for most Divers, their first ride along is an eye-opening experience that changes much of the dialogue. Information and experience are very powerful tools to help us understand each other.

Adapters

Adapters are typically the family members of a loved one with a "normal" job who then enters the field of public safety. Adapters become the family "in tow" into the public safety lifestyle, often without realizing it at first and sometimes without much warning. Adapters are initially exposed to the public safety lifestyle, verbiage, changes in world views, and humor through their public safety professional during the academy.

After graduation from the academy, when a first responder is going through field training, the changes initially seen in the academy are accelerated. Adapters begin to really notice the changes in their first responders and begin to make comments such as "You've changed" quite frequently. This can be a very confusing time because a first responder changes so much in their first year, often without fully realizing how much they have changed. Family members are often confused, concerned, and anxious about these changes but aren't sure how to verbalize it without starting an argument. In these cases, resentment can build, and if family members and first responders are not equipped with the tools to address this, happiness and cohesion at home can begin to deteriorate significantly.

One of the most significant challenges Adapters face during this time is feeling left out. Their first responder has entered a whole new world with a brand-new set of friends, a vocabulary and schedule that has shifted immensely, and a different lifestyle and approach to life. Family members going through this phase can easily become resentful of their first responder's job and the lack of balance they now perceive from their first responder's work and lifestyle versus their home and family.

This is a very difficult phase for family members to experience and tackle. Public safety professionals who are new to the field typically love their jobs wholeheartedly, and they make that very clear. They tend to dominate conversations at home with stories from work and about their shift mates, whom the family may or may not know. They are suddenly bored by and don't want to hear their spouse's stories from work. They can be easily frustrated by their children's tantrums and can lose empathy for family members' bad days because they have now seen so much worse in the line of duty.

Family members going through this can become angry and resentful. They feel as though they cannot compete with the job. At this point, a new challenge also tends to arise for many first responder families—that of finances. At a time when a loved one is feeling left out and resentful, a first responder may begin to make large purchases, given the financial stability of being a public servant. Whether it's extra equipment for work, a vehicle, or an expensive toy such as a new boat, throwing financial issues into the mix becomes gas on the fire.

Adapters also face the challenge of hearing the

stories of their first responders, learning of events on the news, and fearing that something will happen to their loved one. These events can cause fear and anxiety in family members, who then wish their first responder would just return to their "normal" job. When this sentiment is verbalized, many first responders become alarmed and defensive and will change the way they communicate with their family members—by not telling them what they went through, minimizing details, or just completely denying involvement in an incident. The result of this is further divisiveness and less communication at a time when cohesion and communication are vital.

Tips for Adapters

The most important thing for public safety members and family Adapters to understand is that everyone is going through a massive change. While change can be tough, it can also be manageable. The key is to recognize the way things have changed, whether subtle or seismic, and to communicate and work through them. It is okay to seek help as you go through changes as a family. No one is immune to these stressors and getting help is a great way to combat stress.

One of the most important things an Adapter family can do is to go to family night at the Academy, if there is one. This not only gives loved ones the chance to hear about what is ahead for their first responder recruit, it gives family members the chance to ask questions, connect with other family members, and become connected in this community themselves.

Adapters can also benefit from reading literature for both public safety members and family members. Understanding stress, trauma, critical incidents, shift work, the culture, and the lifestyles of public safety personnel increases Adapters' knowledge and insight.

Riding along is an excellent way for Adapter families to understand what it is like for a first responder. I remember a paramedic telling me that his wife told him after a ride along that she would never again question why he was so tired, even on nights when he "got sleep" at the station. This was a beautiful way to bridge the gap between perception and reality and help a spouse understand what it feels like to work a twenty-four-hour shift.

Finally, it is important for first responders and their Adapter families to get help if they need it. When communication is in a vicious cycle and attempts at understanding each other and bridging this gap have failed, and you are out of ideas on how to change things, it is time to get help. The key to getting good help is to seek it from someone who is qualified. Search for someone who has legitimate experience in working with and understanding first responders.

Relationship counseling should be considered a tune-up and should be done as often as needed. If a couple approaches relationship counseling as an overhaul, they will be disappointed. Human beings change gradually and incrementally. Having realistic expectations of change and the understanding that in every relationship there will be quite a bit of negotiating and give and take on both sides is paramount to a couple's success both in counseling and the long run.

Veterans

Veterans are family members who grew up in a public safety family and are now in a relationship with a first responder. This happens quite frequently, as emergency response professions tend to run in families. The philosophy of helping others as a calling is a beautiful mindset that perpetuates itself across generations.

The biggest issue for Veterans is adapting to their role as a significant other or spouse when they grew up a first responder's child. Many Veterans realize just how well their parents did at shielding them from all of the challenges of being a family supporting a public safety professional.

Many Veterans are caught off guard by how many responsibilities they truly have in relation to their non-public safety friends. It is a sharp contrast to other families that requires quite a bit of navigation, especially early on in a relationship when roles and responsibilities are being defined.

The other challenge for Veteran family members is to navigate carefully through the carryover of public safety trauma that occurred when they were children. Being the child of a first responder means that you were exposed to trauma and stress from the job during your childhood, and this is easy to carry into your adult relationship. The impact of this trauma can mean quite a bit of fear, worry, sleepless nights, and overall anxiety.

Tips for Veterans

The biggest thing I ask my Veteran family members to do when they get help for their struggles is to acknowledge how hard this lifestyle can be and to forgive themselves for needing help. We remove the mantra "I should be used to this" and replace it with "It is normal to feel this way and it is okay to need help."

One thing that helps Veterans quite a bit is to jump in and assist the Divers and Adapters. Their words of wisdom, advice, empathy, and normalization are massively helpful for the family members who are new to all of this. It's a total win because the guidance is invaluable and gives Veterans an opportunity to see how much wisdom they have to share, which leads to feelings of fulfillment and accomplishment.

Recently, I was speaking to a group of firefighters' wives and significant others. One wife mentioned how difficult it is when her husband is gone for twenty-four hours at a time. Another wife chimed in and said that this was when she has jurisdiction over the remote control, and every third day she gets to watch what she wants. The wife who was struggling laughed and said how helpful it was to hear another wife's take on things. It really boils down to perspective, and sometimes these pearls of wisdom go a long way in other people's lives.

The Phases of the Public Safety Family

In my book, *Code Four: Surviving and Thriving in Public Safety*, Chapter One highlights the phases of the public safety career. These phases are also true for family members, as public safety families tend to mirror a very similar movement through time and over the years.

Phase One: The Innocence

Early in their careers, public safety professionals tend to be excited, happy, and even exhilarated by their work. Everything is shiny and new, and first responders set out to save lives and help people. There is a sense of innocence that they bring to their work, with very high hopes and sometimes unrealistic expectations.

Family members tend to mirror this phase as well. Families enter into the public safety world with extremely high expectations of their first responder. They tend to think that great things will happen, lives will be saved, and their loved one's career will be marked only by incredible service to others and positive influence on their communities and the people they serve.

Family members in the innocence phase tend to talk about their first responders' work with friends and colleagues and wear clothing such as department t-shirts that shows their support for their first responder. They are proud of their first responder and of their status as a family member.

Phase Two: The End of the Innocence

Usually right around the eight-year mark, first responders reach the end of the innocence phase. They have experienced significantly horrible events and have seen human beings at their worst. They have been exposed to more than their fair share of violence, chaos, and despair. Coinciding with all of this, they have had personal and professional struggles. They have been disciplined and reprimanded. They have been subjected to the politics of the department and have been passed over for promotion or denied access to specialty teams. At the end of the innocence phase, first responders are likely to have burnout, are cynical and angry, and might even be struggling with issues related to trauma.

The family members may share much of the sentiment. They have had multiple Thanksgivings on Wednesday or Friday, Christmas has never been on the 25th of December, and don't forget the soccer season where all of the games lined up perfectly with their first responder being on duty. Family members have also been subjected to the incredibly negative news cycles about first responders and their departments. They have been through critical incidents in the department and with other family members from the department. They have been alienated from friends who perhaps cannot or do not want to understand the lifestyle of a public safety family. Family members at the end of the innocence phase tend to become closed off and isolated almost as much as their public safety loved one does. This is a tough phase for everyone.

At this point, it is imperative to get help. The end of the innocence phase is a very tough phase, and it takes a sharp toll on first responders and family members. Simply taking a day off here and there or going on vacation does not resolve this phase. Just as I explain to first responders, I also educate family members on the fact that they have options at this point. Things can stay the same, they can get worse, or they can improve. I then highlight the importance of achieving the third phase, which is wisdom.

Wisdom

The telltale sign of wisdom is balance. As first responders learn to take a deep breath and take an emotional step back from their work, they achieve wisdom. They go from being overinvested and easily upset by what goes on at work to being much more easy going. They learn to let things go, expend their energy where it matters, and take better care of themselves.

As first responders reach wisdom, they have also begun to resolve their traumas. Through successful care in the counseling realm, public safety personnel can resolve what has occurred in the line of duty by processing the events successfully. In my book, *First Responder Resilience: Caring for Public Servants*, I address trauma and the treatment for traumatic events.

Families must also achieve wisdom through balance. Learning to ignore the media and what people say at work or in the grocery store is vital. Understanding that many people come from a place of a lack of education about first responders is essential to learning to ignore the chatter. Supporting a first responder in their career and also reinvesting in the home life is a hallmark signal of family members who have achieved wisdom. The job becomes less of who they are and more of what they do.

Family members should also be given the opportunity to address the impact of public safety traumas on their lives. Because they are not immune to what goes on around them, family members often experience many of the events themselves and can definitely benefit from the care of qualified counselors.

Wisdom is hard-earned. It causes gray hair. But at the end of it all, first responders and their families have each other, and they have their legacy of living a life in the service of others. There is no greater calling, and family members who make these sacrifices alongside their first responders should be extremely proud of themselves.

Dana's Story

"Hey, honey, how was your day?" Six words I say daily that can begin a conversation or end it before it is even started. As the spouse of a first responder for over twenty-five years, you learn that each day can bring new challenges or revive old memories.

I met my husband when I agreed to a blind date arranged by a coworker. That evening, we shared many laughs at the expense of our mutual friend, but in the end, she knew what she was doing. We connected immediately, and our story began. One commonality we shared was a passion for emergency medicine. I worked in an emergency room, and he was a paramedic with our city's EMS. It did not take me long to learn that although our medical paths crossed, they were also miles apart. I was working in chaos in a controlled environment. He was trying to create a controlled environment out of chaos. I had patients crying over sutures. He was dodging cars and gunfire. While I may be doing chest compressions or splinting a broken arm, he would be finding children and adults deceased or injured in horrific situations.

As a new couple insecure about the strength of our relationship and connection, I did not understand why he would shut down and go silent for brief periods of time. Was it me? Did I do something wrong? Was he just being moody or selfish? Did he have a bad day? Was he just exhausted from his twenty-four-hour or forty-eight-hour shift? Why would he not talk to me about it? These were the questions that I would ask myself each time I saw him slide into a silent phase. Through observation and conversation, I realized early on that our time together was his sanctuary. He needed a place to escape. He needed silence to allow him time to process, decompress, and restore. I had to put my curiosity on the back burner because probing him for details about his shift was counterproductive and possibly even harmful.

A short time after we were married, I can recall a day when reality hit hard. I came home to find my husband curled up on the couch, silent. Mentally and physically he had shut down. He just lay there, his mind haunted by flashes of memories, his body limp from exhaustion. I quietly sat with him, waiting. "What was I waiting for?" you may ask. Honestly, at the time, I was not sure. I did not have answers or solutions, but I wanted him to know that he was not alone. In the mid-90s, PTSD (Post-Traumatic Stress Disorder) was a term that was rarely discussed and then it was only used in reference to military veterans. Those who dated or were married to first responders knew that our partners struggled with the memories of calls, but we did not have a name for it (unless they went into a full depression or became suicidal), nor did we know who to call or how to help them. There was such a stigma surrounding mental health. While some first response employers were trying to institute measures to reduce the number of suicides within the police, fire, and EMS fields, it was still a period when employees believed that raising your hand and flagging down help meant that you were weak and could cost you promotions or even your job.

For me personally, seeing such a vacant look in his

eyes was one of the moments in life that scared me to my core. To me, depression was a darkness that I could not comprehend, but I had seen the extreme outcomes of people who could not overcome it. Now, I could see that depression was like a stalker. It taunts one from the shadows, waiting to overpower them when they least expect it. While I could not fight this battle for him, I did commit to not letting the negative perception of mental health/weakness prevent my husband from getting the professional assistance he needed. I was not going to let a stigma kill him.

We have had an incredible twenty-five-plus years together. He transitioned successfully from the EMS system to the fire department many years ago. Today, he is a leader in the department and our community. Together, we have raised an amazing daughter. That being said, PTSD did not disappear, but we have learned how to manage its effects. Professionally guided EMDR (Eye Movement Desensitization and Reprocessing) therapy and counseling have been key to his success. (Author's note: EMDR is explained in greater detail in my book, *First Responder Resilience: Caring for Public Servants*.) We have learned together how to identify the signs, triggers, and symptoms for maintaining a healthy mental status, both in ourselves and with others. When I see his anxiety or stress levels rising, we stop what we are doing and address it. Sometimes, something as simple as going to the gym can realign the body and mind. Other times, a phone or in-person consultation with a professional is needed. Maintaining a work/life balance is a struggle but has become such a priority that we routinely schedule breaks for weekends of camping/hiking and vacations each year.

Retirement is our next big step. While exciting, this too creates anxiety. We have seen so many first responders struggle with life after retirement. We have observed how these able-bodied (often young) type-A personalities, suddenly free of duties, become bored and then are overcome by a flood of memories and emotions. So how do you reduce the post-retirement shock? You prepare. You make a plan. We have a few years until we take this step, but the key is that discussions of the multiple routes open to our family are on the table.

It is important to acknowledge that PTSD not only affects the first responder, it affects the lives of the entire family too. We, as a family, have learned to slow down or stop to acknowledge the symptoms when they occur. Focusing on mental health wellness has not only strengthened the relationships within our family, but promoting it has assisted others by reducing the stigma that was preventing them from understanding and addressing the needs within their own family and circle of friends.

Chapter Two
Managing the Negative

*I know we're not alright
It's always darkest just before the light
I know your silence is a deadly sound
It's never easy when you're breaking down
But I'll be there when you come around*

"Come Around" by Papa Roach

Inherent in any high-stress occupation such as public safety are the negative effects of the job on first responders and its impacts on family members. While there is no magic answer or one-size-fits-all way to manage through tough times, it is important to be prepared, to be proactive, to communicate as well as you can, and at times to just slow down and take a deep breath.

The main areas that impact families the most seem to be connected with the physical and psychological drains on first responders from their work. From fatigue to trauma, these heavy hitters are by far what the families experience the most.

Shift Work and Fatigue

A chief complaint from first responder family members is how significant the impact of shift work is on their home lives. Public safety personnel walk through the doors of their homes at the end of their shifts completely drained. Their internal fuel tanks are on a solid E for empty, and they are completely void of energy, patience, and a desire to do anything other than sleep or stare at the TV. This happens to coincide with a time when the family may be ready to run errands, get chores done, or for parents, even take a break from dealing with very young children. They've been waiting for their first responder to walk through the front door. It is a perfect mismatch of expectations and energy levels, all under one roof, all at the same time. This is a tough thing to navigate, given how busy lives can be with the demands of schedules and high expectations that we have for each other.

The key to managing this is to find your family rhythm through navigating the impact of shift work on first responders and finding the happy medium between an empty internal fuel tank and the needs of a busy family system. In other words, acknowledge and understand the mismatch of energy and life rhythm, and work through it.

The first thing to understand is the impact of shift work on first responders. As the uniform goes on toward the beginning of the shift, first responders typically are focused on what's ahead. They may be watching the news, listening to their work radio, or checking in with on-duty crews. As they head out the door, safety and non-complacency become the priority. In order to do this, situational awareness is vital. Everything in a worst-case scenario boils down to being prepared, muscle memory, and training. Being caught off guard or behind the curve during a dangerous incident is every first responder's worst nightmare.

What this means is that most first responders are already in what I call a "low-grade fever level of fight or flight" before they even leave the house. Their bodies have already started producing more adrenaline, glucose, and cortisol as they hit the streets or enter their stations. Throughout the shift, as calls come in, first responders will ride the fight-or-flight wave throughout the duration of their duty time. If a certain call is dangerous or extremely difficult, public safety personnel can and will enter full-blown fight or flight and maintain it for as long as they need to.

Because they are riding the fight-or-flight wave throughout a shift, first responders tend to feel great. They are energized, witty, and happy. This is short-lived, because the brain and body will only maintain this for as long as it needs to.

At the end of the shift, on the drive home, first responders hit the adrenaline "dump." As the brains of first responders determine that they are safe, they tell the body to let off the fight-or-flight response because it is no longer necessary. For most first responders, this occurs as they are pulling into their neighborhood or when they are about three miles from their homes if they live in a rural area.

As your first responder is walking in the door, their energy is crashing. They will comment about how tired they are, how they don't want to make any decisions, how they want to be left alone. This is an actual physical withdrawal they are going through, and it is just as much a part of every shift as the ramp-up is when they are on their way to work.

For family members, this is not fun or easy to navigate. Families frequently express frustration about how energized and happy their first responder is at work and how angry and withdrawn they are at home. Family members are on the receiving end of grumpy, withdrawn, depressed, and angry first responders.

The key here is to not take this personally and to allow for the necessary rebound or rally time that your first responder needs. This means that as a couple, you communicate about the best way to navigate through this cycle.

First responders who work twenty-four-hour or forty-eight-hour shifts must take a nap on their first day off. "Sleeping" at a fire or EMS station is not like sleeping in your own bed. First responders who have this down time are dressed in work clothes, in a bed that is not their own, listening for tones to drop for calls and worried they will sleep through a call. Typically, they wake up multiple times. In no way is this a good rest. Whether your first responder needs a nap right away when they walk in the door or sometime around midday, allowing for this will create a much better day for everyone. The maximum amount of nap time should be a conscious choice. I never recommend that first responders sleep all day, because this disrupts the sleep patterns by hindering going to bed at a normal time that night.

For first responders who work eight-, ten-, or twelve-hour shifts, I recommend a nap on the first day of their consecutive days off. Again, this type of sleep is restorative and healthy. Working multiple shifts like this back-to-back typically translates to little down time, short nights and, by the end of the work week, significant sleep deprivation.

One of the biggest challenges in all of this is having small children. I have worked with first responders who flip their circadian rhythm from working nights to caring for children during the day on their days off, and I have even worked with first responders who work all night and only sleep when their child naps during the day while their spouse is at work. This is a very tough time for couples and the exhaustion is significant. I ask these couples to do the best they can in allowing each other to get necessary sleep and to ask for help from family members and babysitters as often as they can. Fortunately, this phase does not last forever, but it sure can test the sanity of the entire family.

Another important aspect of fatigue has to do with the high volume of stress and stress responses in first responders. When my patients present with anything sounding remotely like depression or anxiety, the first thing I ask them to do is visit their physician and get blood work done. Specifically, I am looking at their cortisol, Vitamin D, testosterone (even in females), and their thyroid. I jokingly refer to first responders as "chemical nightmares" because in my practice we are finding that eight out of ten first responders are producing lab work with one or more of these levels in the unhealthy range. This is significant because it impacts energy and mood tremendously. Many of my customers have now added these panels to annual physicals. This is a great way to get a baseline and monitor how things are changing.

Trauma

Whether accidents or acts of malice, man-made or natural disasters, events with warning or those without any at all, it is likely that most first responders will face multiple traumas throughout their careers. As first responders are faced with unfathomable pain, despair, and horror, they carry the burden to stop the problem, save lives, impart justice, and clean up the mess. In Chapter Three, I will address the impact of trauma on family members. In this chapter, I want to place tools in the toolboxes of family members so they know what to do for their first responder.

Traumatic events are usually sudden and extreme. They overwhelm the usual coping capacities of first responders. It is important to note, however, that what one person considers traumatic might be nontraumatic for someone else. When my team works in the aftermath of a trauma, we deliberately put our fingers on the emotional pulses of all first responders involved so we can get a sense of each individual's interpretation.

Interpretation is based on one's history, training, prior experience, successful resolution of previous situations, and perspective. It is unique to each person. It is not uncommon for one first responder to tell me, "This is the worst thing I have ever seen" while another says, "Been there. Done that. These things happen."

When a person is exposed to trauma that is beyond their human coping capacity, the data—the sights, smells, sounds, tactile feelings, and even taste, whatever is impacted—gets stored in the frontal lobe of the brain. The brain's frontal lobe serves as a firewall during trauma, and it captures what first responders see, hear, taste, touch, and smell. The frontal lobe does this because at the time of the trauma, it simply cannot process this information as though it is normal, not to mention the fact that the first responder is way too busy at the time to truly process an event.

What happens next is the replay—this is when a first responder replays the event over and over again, as though it is a movie in the mind. They see, hear, taste, touch, and smell the event, as though it is still happening. First responders will remark how the smell won't leave their nose. Or they will seem distracted and distant as they replay the event again and again. They may have nightmares or even night terrors. What is happening is the frontal lobe is handing the first responder all of the sights, smells, and sounds in an attempt to process the event. Basically, the brain is telling the first responder that this event has to be dealt with. Although not pleasant, this is very normal for the first few days.

The best thing for first responders to do at this point is it to talk about what has happened with someone they trust, be it a colleague, someone from their peer support team, a family member, clergy, or a counselor. I always tell public safety personnel that they do not have to talk about their feelings, just talk through it. The more they talk, especially in the first few days, the more their brains will begin to "download" the event into their long-term memory. Writing is another way to process the trauma. For first responders who are so inclined, the ability to journal about what they are going through is a very effective way to process trauma.

The next phase is critical. What I always tell first responders is that over the next few days, we want the call to start to fade. By seven days post-incident, we want our public safety personnel to describe the event as though it is fading to their long-term memory. In other words, they still think about the event or call frequently, but the replay is nowhere near as bad as it was on the first few days. Over the following seven days, we want this fading to continue. This means that by fourteen days post-incident, first responders describe the event as being in their long-term memory versus right in their face. The fading means the healthy, resilient brain is processing this call and moving it from the frontal lobe, where it is not supposed to be stored, to the long-term memory, where we want it to be stored.

If, at fourteen days, a first responder feels as though they have not recovered or experienced significant fading, it is important to get competent help. At this point, everything we do clinically for a first responder is preventative. Being distressed at two weeks post-incident is considered Post-Traumatic Stress (PTS) and not Post-Traumatic Stress Disorder (PTSD). Post-Traumatic Stress is a normal and adaptive response to experiencing trauma. Getting good care at this point will likely mitigate the impact of the event. It also gives health care providers the ability to monitor a first responder and assure that the trauma is not progressing to Post-Traumatic Stress Disorder.

The difference between trauma and a bad memory is that trauma stays in the frontal lobe and triggers a person indefinitely until they get help. A bad memory is just that—it's a fading, distant memory that can be accessed if someone chooses to, and it does not produce the types of triggers that send the individual into unnecessary fight-or-flight responses. First responders who have good training, a solid history of coping well, and healthy avenues for stress relief are considered resilient. The more resilient a first responder is, the more likely they will be able to cope effectively with an incident, within reason. Everyone, no matter how tough or experienced they are, has a limit to how much trauma they can endure.

Family members should understand that it is often very difficult for first responders to talk about their trauma. Whether they learned falsely from someone that they are weak for being impacted, don't know how to put what they are experiencing into words, are afraid if they say something they will lose their jobs, or are afraid of traumatizing their family members, first responders frequently keep traumas to themselves. Unfortunately, this leads to many years of suffering and unnecessary pain for many people.

Encouraging first responders to share what they can in an environment that is free of judgment and criticism is one of the best ways for family members to get their public safety personnel to open up. Educating them on the seven- and fourteen-day progress timelines is also very important, because it gives first responders some guidelines for getting help.

The bottom line is that trauma impacts everyone. It does not have to be this awful beast that destroys first responders and simultaneously or subsequently their family members. We embrace the event; we tackle the demons and provide good help so that first responders can restore their equilibrium and their resilience. In my book, *First Responder Resilience: Caring for Public Servants*, I describe Post-Traumatic Stress Disorder in full detail, along with options for effective trauma treatment.

Suicide

Suicide is a very scary and tough subject to talk about. The act of taking one's life has ripple effects beyond comprehension. It is heartbreaking to hear of the helpers being so overwhelmed that they take their own lives. It just should not be this way.

In studying suicide, we know that either depression or bipolar disorder is present in almost all individuals who take their own lives. In diagnosing depression, we look at three key factors: anhedonia, which means lack of joy (i.e., not finding joy in anything), changes in eating patterns, and changes in sleeping patterns for a two-week duration. The onset of depression is a slow simmer to a boil. For many people, they have lived and coped with it for so long, they no longer remember what it feels like to feel good. They can access zero positive memories, and it is hard to see the big picture in terms of what they are dealing with.

For first responders, as we look at the challenges they face, we are beginning to realize some important points to address in conjunction with depression. The copious fight-or-flight responses—shift after shift, year after year—are creating significant issues with the balance of glucocorticoids and adrenal fatigue in first responders. Additionally, the lack of sleep that first responders typically endure is putting gas on the fire. If we push someone hard enough with no sleep, they will become psychotic. When you combine adrenal fatigue and sleep deprivation together, it is a recipe for disaster.

The most important thing to realize is to get help. As a family member, if your first responder is struggling, offer to go to counseling with them. An appointment with a counselor that is a family event versus going by oneself is frequently far less threatening or intimidating. Once rapport is established with a therapist, first responders are more likely to consider going by themselves and then the care can continue.

Resilience

Achieving and maintaining resilience is a life-long process that first responders and their family members should focus on. Resilience means living the best life possible and functioning at the best level possible. No one is perfectly resilient.

Resilience building starts with the basics: hydration, nutrition, rest, and exercise. When I teach, I explain to audiences that small changes in these areas pay off big. In other words, you start to see and feel results, and it motivates you to continue. Setting small and achievable goals is the key here.

I am not a fan of New Year's resolutions because

they tend to be vague and unachievable. Rather than a New Year's resolution of "getting into shape" or "losing weight," I ask first responders and their family members who are setting fitness goals to simply move their bodies more. My manta is, "Do what you love, just move your body." My other mantra is, "If running hurts your knees, I don't want you to run." In other words, start with what you will succeed at, set reasonable goals, and have fun doing it.

We build on resilience by addressing life outside the job—family, faith, friends, and hobbies. Because public safety is a culture and a lifestyle, first responders sometimes forget they are allowed to have lives, friends, and hobbies that have nothing to do with work! Again, small changes pay off big. Reconnecting with old friends, carving out date nights, and enjoying the quality time you build for yourself really helps refuel that inner fuel tank!

Resilience also includes altruism and gratitude. Because of the work first responders do, they typically have very high altruistic markers in their personalities. Gratitude means counting your blessings and taking note of the positives. This is difficult during tough times but important to maintain the big picture. In my book, *First Responder Resilience: Caring for Public Servants*, I wrote extensively on resilience and resilience-building. First responders and their families should take the time to invest in resilience and to consider it a work in progress.

Tara's Story

Ryan and I met in the spring of 2008, dated for two years, and have now been married for nine years. We love spending time together and thrive when we are outdoors, hiking, running, mountain biking, and skiing. With him as a firefighter and myself as a Neonatal ICU nurse, we are both passionate about being in the "helper" field. The beauty of our relationship has always been that we understand each other and recognize that each of us experience joy, trauma, and sadness at our places of work and, for us, being able to share our experiences helps us to cope with situations.

Four years into our marriage, I got pregnant with our daughter, Sawyer. Right from the start, it turned out to be a difficult pregnancy filled with weekly appointments, bed rest, and an early delivery. Sawyer was born with a very rare genetic syndrome that causes physical differences and, quite honestly, blindsided us. I dealt with my grief immediately, struggling through the first year, carried by Ryan and my family. I always remarked that Ryan was my rock, being able to face specialists' appointments with a clear head, being present for Sawyer and me, while continuing to work full time as a firefighter. We made it through all of the procedures Sawyer had to have, returned to our active lifestyle, started to travel, and really felt like things were finally okay.

Then I feel like Ryan had his turn. The first difference I noticed in Ryan was that he stopped sharing. He would come home from the station, and I would ask how his shift was, and rather than tell me about the calls, he would say, "It was fine, nothing much to tell." And that was it. While he had always been a good sleeper, he started sleeping for twelve to fourteen hours and still woke up feeling exhausted. At first, I just assumed he had been running lots of calls during the night and shifts were wearing on him, but then he would say he didn't run any calls and slept all night at the station. It didn't add up. Gradually he started gaining a little weight and stopped wanting to ride his bike or go on runs with me. We enjoyed hiking as a family and carrying Sawyer in the backpack, but it was a struggle to get him interested in doing that. Initially my goal was to get him motivated to be active again, work on his diet, and see if that helped with his sleep and energy. Then he started withdrawing more. He would be sitting with us or trying to play with Sawyer but would just stare into space and not truly be present. He stopped doing things around the house as much and just sat on the couch with his phone. A phrase I frequently use is "think out loud," trying to get him to share whatever was occupying his thoughts so much, and he would tell me he wasn't thinking about anything. Already during these times, I had suggested maybe he talk to someone if he felt like he was struggling, and he was reluctant at first. Then we planned a vacation to Hawaii, and I was sure that time away from work would be the trick to knock him out of the funk, but it wasn't. Then his attitude changed again. He was quick to anger, easily frustrated at home and work, and even his relationship with Sawyer was changing. He kept saying no matter what he tried, he felt like he could never focus. At that point, we had the hard talk about how this was not the Ryan I knew, something was going on, please talk to someone. Finally, he agreed.

It took a few weeks, but he came home one day and told me that his department offered therapy through a particular practice that worked specifically with first responders. He struggled with that first call of making an appointment and how much information to give over the phone or what to ask for, but he did it. I wish I could say after his first session that he felt a weight off his chest and felt so much better, but I remember him getting home and being devastated that not only did he not feel better but he felt worse and hopeless. He said, "We didn't even talk about Sawyer!" I told him that he couldn't get through everything in one session and his therapist needed to get to know him and ask all the things and eventually he would get there, so he reluctantly went back for a second session. After the third or fourth session, I could tell he and his therapist had developed a rapport, and he was starting to look forward to his talks with him. Around the same time, Ryan finally told me about a call that he hadn't told me about from the past spring that he couldn't get out of his head, which was around the time all of these behaviors triggered. It was a heartbreaking CPR call on a little girl that reminded him of Sawyer. I asked him why he didn't tell me about it when it happened, and he said he didn't want to upset me and it hit too close to home. This was when he said that his therapist recommended EMDR treatment.

It was New Year's Eve, and we were out to eat when he was telling me about his EMDR session and said he felt better, like a weight lifted off his shoulders. But he was still skeptical about whether or not it really worked or was just a placebo. I remember asking, "Do you feel better?" And he said, "Yes." And I said, "Then does it matter?"

What he discovered during his sessions was that he was trying to focus on the CPR call but really what he kept thinking about and seeing was our daughter's delivery and resuscitation, her lying on a hospital bed with IVs and oxygen after surgeries, and all of the visits to different doctors for her. While the call had indeed been traumatic for him, what it had really triggered was the trauma from the past four years with Sawyer that he had never really dealt with.

As first responders, they are not only witnessing the worst days of some people's lives on a daily basis but are required to cope with these events on their own while dealing with stressors in their own lives. It's a lot to bear. While EMDR wasn't a quick fix in itself, combined with talk therapy, it made all the difference. Eventually, he started sleeping better, eating better, talking more, and here we are a year later and he's back to being active again! We are both very grateful for the services offered and glad that more departments are utilizing and promoting this practice!

Chapter Three
Vicarious Trauma

Why do I still feel so lost?
Why do I still seem out of place?
Everyone's out of focus
Everything blurry looks the same

"Blurry (Out of Place)" by Crown the Empire

"This didn't happen directly to me! Why am I impacted so much and why am I struggling?"

This phrase is the telltale sign of vicarious trauma. It's the impact of being exposed to someone else's traumas, coupled with the internal struggle of shame and guilt over being impacted so strongly by a trauma that may not be our own. Because it's not our own, somehow we feel that we don't have the right to be impacted. Welcome to vicarious trauma—it's very real, it's awful, and it's important to manage.

What Is Vicarious Trauma?

Vicarious trauma, also known as secondary trauma, is

the emotional impact and residue as a result of being exposed to other people's traumas. The exposure to the trauma can be as indirect as hearing someone's account of what happened to them.

While vicarious trauma has typically been a concept applied to helpers—law enforcement, fire service, emergency medical services, dispatchers, medical professionals, mental health professionals, hospice workers, and social workers—we know that vicarious trauma can and will impact anyone who has a significant relationship with a survivor. The legal professions are now even considering the impact of vicarious trauma on attorneys, judges, and jurors. This type of trauma is real, and it is valid.

Hearing someone's story, especially when one is close emotionally to a trauma survivor, can overwhelm a person. When vicarious trauma sets in, the person hearing a story can take on the same reactions to a lesser extent as the survivor.

The emotional symptoms of vicarious trauma include lasting feelings of grief, sadness, anger, and isolation. Vicarious trauma can also cause feelings of helplessness and resentment.

The behavioral changes of vicarious trauma include changes in eating and sleeping patterns, increased use of alcohol, and avoiding certain people or situations. Sometimes people experiencing vicarious trauma will engage in risk-taking behavior.

While many people have the ability to override

their stress by mentally compartmentalizing their trauma, the body has an amazing way of showing just how stressed or traumatized a person is. Headaches, rashes, heartburn, and ulcers are a few of the ways people respond physically to vicarious trauma.

A very negative outlook, cynicism, difficulty concentrating, and difficulty making decisions are the typical cognitive signs of vicarious trauma. Along with this, a person may have a very difficult time not thinking about the trauma and therefore may struggle with focusing both at work and at home.

Finally, spiritually, a person suffering from vicarious trauma may experience a loss of hope and purpose. They may also experience a feeling of disconnectedness and may even lose sight of their life purpose.

First Responder Families and Vicarious Trauma

First responder families are often subjected to vicarious trauma in two ways. In my work, I have identified these by using the terms "Indirect Vicarious Trauma" and "Direct Vicarious Trauma."

Indirect Vicarious Trauma

Indirect vicarious trauma occurs for loved ones of emergency services personnel when a first responder takes a call or deals with a situation that impacts them by striking a personal chord. The first responder is faced with vicarious trauma, and they then carry the impact home.

This is when the family is affected.

Typically, what happens in the work life of emergency services personnel is they take call after call, shift after shift, and are not impacted emotionally by the work they do. This is the result of experience, training, and perspective gained through good mentorship and the fact that there is just not enough time or energy to be impacted personally by these situations. Then, suddenly and unexpectedly, the high-impact call comes in, first responders jump in to help, and are met with a wave of unanticipated emotion due to the nature of the event.

These events are typically ones involving children because kids garner so much emotion. Children are helpless and we value them intensely. The serious injury to or loss of a child is one of our greatest fears, so calls involving children are extremely difficult.

There are many other types of situations that impact first responders. It might be an assault survivor, a veteran, an elderly person, a physically handicapped person, or a person struggling with mental illness. Because public safety personnel see people on the worst days of their lives, they often see despair and intense suffering or sadness. One tiny detail of any call where a first responder makes a personal connection creates a window for vicarious trauma.

The indirect vicarious trauma on the family members occurs when the first responder brings the emotional impact of the call home. Many public safety professionals have shared with me all of the behaviors they exhibited after these types of calls, as well as how it impacted their families. The most typical behaviors we see in first responders are nitpicking their loved ones, extreme hypervigilance during family activities, and loss of control of anger over seemingly innocuous situations.

I have worked with countless first responders after vicarious trauma. First responders often tell me how when they get home after a really tough child death, they can't stop hugging their kids to the point that eventually the kids even get irritated. Other first responders have told me that they cannot look at their kids because they are so saddened by the situation that they feel incredible guilt and sorrow when they do.

Then there are the 3 a.m. calls. First responders have mentioned doing things like calling their spouse in the middle of the night to make sure the baby is breathing after a SIDS death. They call to make sure the doors and windows are locked after working a sexual assault where the perpetrator came through an unlocked door. Many loved ones initially argue and will say things like, "Yes, of course the baby is breathing" or "Yes, I locked the door! Why are you calling me in the middle of the night?"

Over time, though, with experience, communication, and understanding, loved ones tend to change their response. They will check the windows and doors, check on the baby, or make sure the smoke detector works because they now understand. Many times, with the wisdom that spouses have gained from these experiences, they learn to say the right things to include their "couple code words" of love and support to reassure their first responder that what is happening out there in the world is not happening in the sanctity of their home.

Direct Vicarious Trauma

Direct vicarious trauma is awful. It is the painful direct exposure to another human being's suffering and can significantly impact a person's mental and physical heath.

For public safety families, direct vicarious trauma occurs when there is a line-of-duty death or serious injury. During these times, first responders are beside themselves—they are impacted so significantly by the trauma, grief, and aftermath of this type of situation that it bleeds over and directly impacts their loved ones.

During these times, many family members will report that they are experiencing anxiety, fear, insomnia, nightmares, confusion, and many other cognitive, emotional, and physical manifestations of stress. Many times, family members will also comment that they don't understand why they are responding this way since they are not directly impacted. This type of vicarious trauma is completely legitimate, is understandable, and warrants care for family members just as much as for the first responders.

Family members are frequently very "in tune" with each other. Couples are impacted by each other's stressors and when very turbulent times hit, it is normal for loved ones to manifest the same symptoms as the first responder. As soon as they walk in the door, family members experience the pain and stress of the situation. They fear this type of event will happen to their loved one. They begin to imagine worst-case scenarios, and this can lead to some very disruptive circular thought patterns and fears.

To add to this, in every awful situation that hits a person or an agency, public safety family members always kick in to help the impacted public safety professional and/or their family members. It is ingrained in public safety family members that they are all family, so helping out is an automatic drive for them. This means family members suddenly fill the role of trauma counselor, grief counselor, babysitter for very upset children, meal planner, chauffer, errand runner, and whatever else needs to get done at the time.

Throughout this entire time, family members are exposed to significantly painful circumstances and emotions. Most family members will do what they need to in order to support the impacted personnel and their families. During this time, they will typically shelve their feelings and reactions and maintain a position of strength and support. It is imperative that agencies, peer support teams, mental health professionals, and anyone else involved in picking up the pieces that they not discount or exclude the family members.

Overcoming vicarious trauma is essential for good mental health. It is imperative to ask for help when needed and to seek counseling from a qualitied mental health provider. If someone is struggling and they do nothing to seek assistance, the impact on that person's health, family, and life can be very negative.

I personally have a passionate stance on vicarious trauma, as I went through this myself in the aftermath of my deployment to Oklahoma City after the bombing of the Murrah Building in 1995. I was a very young clinician, and this was my first major disaster. I was doing pretty well that week until I was separated from the peer support team I deployed with. I was put on a special assignment and was privileged to work with several members of the morgue crew. I sat with these amazing people for several hours. They were very traumatized. I listened to their stories of what they did as a team from start to finish. They were soon to return home, and all I could do was beg them to get help. I had so little time with them other than our few hours together. At the end they hugged me and thanked me. I remember thinking that I did not know why they were thanking me, because I felt so helpless and as though I had not done enough for them.

When I rejoined my peer support team later that day, one of the paramedics asked how I was doing and of course I told him I was fine. He commented that I had the thousand-yard stare, and my reply was to ask him where we were going for the next assignment.

I returned home completely numb. I remember thinking how different everything felt. I went back to my city, my home, and my job feeling completely foreign and out of sorts. I refer to this feeling as "a stranger in a strange land."

The real struggle was when I returned to work. At the time I worked in a Level II trauma center, and my shift was weekend nights. In my first few minutes of my first shift back, I was yelling at a doctor about how the nineteen-year-old who "overdosed" on an antibiotic was "complete bullshit and a waste of time." I was not okay. As a matter of fact, I was a complete wreck. Like most hard chargers, I pressed on. I did all the right things—I worked out harder, I ran more miles, I ate really well, I avoided alcohol. Nothing worked. Nothing changed.

I struggled for months with compassion fatigue. My attitude was terrible, and I always felt tired. I had a constant knot in my stomach. I had visited with several doctors about the constant stomachache I had, and no one could figure out what was wrong.

Six months after my return from Oklahoma City, in a moment of frustration and basically being done with my attitude, one of the ER nurses confronted me in a loving, ER nurse kind of way. She told me that ever since I had returned from Oklahoma City, I was "a complete asshole." She told me that I needed help. She commented that she did not know if it was PTSD or something else, since she did not understand what I went through in Oklahoma City, but she made sure to reiterate that whatever it was, I definitely needed help.

This was a pivotal point in my life and my career.

At the time I was considering walking away from a career I had once loved tremendously. I am so glad this nurse-tough-love moment happened because I got help.

I jumped into therapy with a great therapist who helped restore my balance and resilience. Then one day, during a clinical supervision hour, I was talking to my supervisor about a case I had while on duty in the ER when suddenly the words "Did I ever tell you about the morgue crew in OKC?" came tumbling out of my mouth. My supervisor's chin dropped and everything else came tumbling out of me. The sadness, the helplessness, and most importantly, my guilt. I refer to this as emotional vomiting. I told her everything, and she did not hesitate to tell me that I did my job and I did everything I could for them. Between therapy and the mentorship of supervision, I healed. I learned about my limits, and I regained balance in my life.

Today, my experience in Oklahoma City has made me a better clinician, public speaker, and person. I am so glad I didn't leave this amazing career I love so much.

An Amazing Public Safety Family

I am honored to finish this chapter with three submissions from a beautiful public safety family. The first piece is titled "Things I Know," written by a retired police chief. I used his story in my book, *Code Four: Surviving and Thriving in Public Safety*. He came to our practice a year before his retirement because he wanted to do it right. He wanted to live happily and enjoy the rest of his life without dragging the demons of trauma with him. He accepted all the help we could offer, and he is doing great. His work is followed by two accounts of vicarious trauma from his wife and his daughter, who is now a law enforcement officer's wife. They both went through amazingly and eerily similar experiences. I absolutely adore this family and everything they stand for.

William: "Things I Know"

Things I know… that I wish I didn't.

I know that large quantities of blood smell like copper and large quantities of fear taste like metal.

I know what almost every kind of dead person looks like. Young, old, middle-aged, shot, stabbed, blown up, run over, hanged, drowned, mangled, dismembered, inside, outside, fresh that died while I watched and dead so long that they don't resemble a person any longer.

I know that grief has many sounds. Wails, sobs, roars, groans, whimpers, and that sometimes grief is so big that you just sit and rock.

I know that you can cuss and pray and fight all at the same time.

I know a simple test to tell if an inarticulate toddler has been violated.

I know what hatred and madness and racism looks like when I see it looking at me from the eyes of another human.

I know how to read the small signs of habitual violence when I walk into a home.

I know what a person looks like when they have had enough of life and hope has left them.

I know what it looks like when a person is guilty and pretends they are not.

I know the look of fear and longing in my loved ones' eyes when I get called out for an emergency.

I know what it sounds like when one human strikes another with a hand, a fist, a stick.

I know what it looks like when you can't find your child or your elderly parent.

I know what it looks like when you finally realize that your loved one loves beer or dope more than anything or anyone else.

I know what it feels like to fight with men who have shot themselves in the head and are trying to reload or get to a bigger gun.

I know what it feels like to drive so fast to come help you that I wreck my car so badly that I can't come help you.

I know the sound of angry, killing gunfire as well as the sound of a gun fired in despair. I also know the sound of rescuing gunfire.

I know what it feels like to be misunderstood and have my actions judged by those who don't understand what I can and cannot do.

These are things that I know because of my love

for you. These are things that I know because of my service to you. I don't regret knowing these things, because along with the things that I wish I didn't know, I have things that I'm very glad I know.

I'm glad that I know the sound of families having a good time out in the yard—laugher, music—as I patrol.

I'm glad that I know the sounds of life returning after CPR was administered.

I'm glad I know what it looks like to see you waving at me as I follow up a parade, as I pass you on the road, as I am sitting in my front yard.

I'm glad that I know what it feels like to have you hug me and to shake my hand and say, "Thank you" from the depths of your being.

I'm glad that I know the surprised feeling when I get to the cash register and learn that some unknown someone—you—bought my lunch.

I'm glad that I know what it feels like to be connected in a community that is seemingly made up of "every tribe, tongue, and nation" and that most of the time, most of us get along remarkably well as we heal and grow and recover from sins committed by our forefathers.

I'm glad that I know what it feels like to find what was taken from you and bring it back to you.

I'm glad that I know what it feels like to be a small part of the very long process of healing when another human has done something to hurt you.

I'm glad I know that good feeling when sometimes I had extra money and I was able to pay your traffic warrant when you couldn't pay it.

I'm glad I know what it feels like to come carry you and your children through the high water, what it feels like to make a difference in your life.

Love led me into a career in law enforcement. Love helped me transition into a peace-keeper. And, finally, Love led me out and back to my truest, quietest self. Wherever Love leads next, I'll be stumbling along behind Him, at Peace.

Rhanda's Story

On June 18, 1998, I experienced the knock on the door that every LEO (law enforcement officer) wife fears. My husband didn't die that night, but my hopes for a long life together did.

Bill had been a peace officer for eight years at the time and was on patrol when the phone rang just after midnight. It was my husband, who quickly said he was okay, but his partner had been shot. The call lasted less than a minute.

I shot out of a deep sleep and immediately called my sister-in-law, another LEO wife, and told her what had happened. I asked her to come over to stay with our kids, ages six, five, and two, so I could go to the hospital and help the officer's wife. I had met the wife for the first time the previous week when our families had dinner together. I assumed she was at the hospital and might need help with their two-year-old daughter.

When I arrived at the hospital, police cars were everywhere, and two officers were standing outside. I asked them where I could find the officer's wife and child. They looked at me with dumfounded expressions and said nothing. I repeated the question and added that I wanted to take the child home with me so the wife could be with her husband. Again, they just stared at me, and finally said, "He didn't make it."

I was shocked... somehow, I just thought he was shot in the toe or something minor. It had never entered my mind that his injury was fatal. "Where is his wife?" I asked, and again, I got blank stares and silence. She wasn't at the hospital. She had not been told anything. She was totally unaware of the awful event that had occurred. "She needs to know! Someone has to tell her!" I was enraged on her behalf, and when it was finally time to go tell her, the officers took me along. I followed their patrol cars to a home on a quiet tree-lined street and parked in front of a small home.

Standing on the porch in the wee hours of the morning of that dark, dark day, my heart was pounding as it was also breaking, and fear overtook my mind. I saw the look on that wife's face when she answered the knock on her door, and I experienced the worst nightmare of every law enforcement officer spouse, even though it was not my husband.

In that moment, I knew exactly what it would be

like WHEN, not if, the knock would be heard on my door. In that moment, I lost hope that I would live a long life with my husband. In that moment, fear settled in my heart.

I grabbed the little girl from the wife's arms and walked inside the house. Determination became my goal, and I was going to be strong for the wife, for the daughter, for my husband, for our children. I was going to be strong, despite the quivering in my heart. I was going to be strong.

The next few days were a blur. I stayed on the couch with the little girl the rest of the night, praying over her, and singing to her as she slept in my arms. I remember going home and later returning to the wife's home with a jar of pickles and offers to help in any way I could. I attended the funeral and stood with the immediate family during the services. I drove to the cemetery, which was hours away, and then suddenly I was home again, ready to get back to normal. But I was never quite the same after that knock on the door.

For the next twenty years, my husband and I dealt with the fallout of that night in our own ways. Our marriage miraculously stayed strong and the deep love we have for one another continued to carry us through the years, even though I secretly planned his funeral over and over and over. Our children grew up in a happy home and went off to college and eventually all got married, while I continued to secretly plan how I would grieve his inevitable death and then continue to live.

Grandchildren arrived and all looked to be grand in our home, but deep down inside, I was unable to look beyond the immediate good day we were living and see a real future with my husband. I was always waiting for the knock on the door, and I was always planning his funeral.

I didn't believe we would be able to grow old together. I didn't want to plan things too far out into the future. I didn't have the hope of a long life with him, even after he retired from law enforcement after a twenty-seven-year, ten-month career. My fears turned from the inevitable knock to fears of cancer or accidents. I truly couldn't see a future with him. I was living a life of grief. I had experienced an end-of-life notice on that porch and I couldn't let it go.

And then I got help. Enter Dr. Tania Glenn! What a gift she has and shares. Talking to her and going through EMDR changed my entire outlook on life with my husband. She helped me experience the trauma and look at all of the pieces of that day and the subsequent years logically instead of only emotionally. I was able to process and put away the fear, and I am thrilled to say that my thoughts about the future INCLUDE my husband and dreams of the two of us growing VERY OLD together, and always living the love that we have never let die.

And because apparently lightning strikes twice in the same family...

Kelly's Story

On Saturday, August 31, 2019, I received the phone call that no law enforcement officer's wife ever wants to receive. My husband had been a Texas State Trooper in Midland for eleven months. He was out on a routine patrol when he called to interrupt my FaceTime session with my mom and my six-month-old son who was staying with my parents. Our phone call lasted less than thirty seconds. It was short, brief, and certainly to the point. My husband stated, "I'm okay, but Chuck has been shot, please call Bridget. I'm okay, but please call Bridget." He hung up the phone, and the sirens were still ringing in my ears.

I quickly got up and walked out the door to my car, dialing Bridget's number on the way. I couldn't breathe while the phone was ringing, my heart was pounding, and I wasn't sure what I was going to say to her. How do I tell someone that their husband has been shot in the line of duty? It's the one phone call we all pray we never receive. She answered, and I could hear her crying on the other side of the phone, and I heaved a sigh of relief that I was not the one who had to deliver the news. I was the second person who called her, and I told her that I was on my way to the hospital, and I started to pray with her. I told her to breathe and not hang up until she got to the hospital.

Upon arrival at the hospital, I was informed that

there was still an active shooter, which meant that my husband was still out there. I pushed those thoughts aside as I saw Bridget and her eight-year-old son walk through the hospital doors. I dug deep and put a smile on my face. From that moment on, I knew that I wanted to help her in any way I could. I wanted to be there for her 100 percent, no matter what.

Bridget was allowed to go back into the ER to see her husband, while I sat in the waiting room with their son. I honestly cannot explain how difficult it was to have chit-chat or small talk with an eight-year-old, when it was obvious that we were both thinking of other things.

Eventually we were also allowed back into the ER, and it was total chaos. I am a first responder. I serve as an Emergency Medical Technician on a 911 ambulance service, and I was completely overwhelmed with the amount of activity happening in the ER. I kept an eye on Bridget while she quietly listened to all that the multiple doctors were telling her. Occasionally she would ask me, "What did they say? I can't remember," and I would repeat what they had said. I felt like I was having an out-of-body experience being there in that situation. No, it wasn't my husband, but it was still one of my family members. It was one of us, a law enforcement officer's wife standing there while her husband was lying in a hospital bed.

After they took the trooper up for surgery, one of the nurses handed his bloody boots to his wife. She turned pale and gingerly placed her hand on them to take them. I stepped in and asked for a bag to place them in. I was shocked that they would simply hand those over to his wife.

The rest of the time in the hospital was a blur; at one point while the trooper was in surgery, my husband finally showed up, and he looked exhausted. All of the troopers had the same blank stare on their faces. I had no idea how I was going to be strong enough to provide support for him as well. I wanted to make sure my husband knew that he could rely on me and be vulnerable with me throughout this process of recovery.

People were coming and going, shaking hands and offering condolences. All the while, I was there next to Bridget, offering my support and encouragement. Once her husband made it out of surgery, another trooper's wife and I followed Bridget home to get fresh clothes and shower to prepare for the days ahead. While Bridget was packing, we decided to go ahead and clean up the trooper's uniform the best we could. I was standing there in the kitchen washing blood off of his name badge and his state trooper badge, thinking, "When is this going to be my husband? When will it be my turn to stand in the hospital waiting?" I pushed my thoughts down and continued with the task at hand.

Over the next few days, I spent countless hours at the hospital quietly sitting with Bridget, helping her delegate tasks to troopers, making sure that she ate and drank appropriately and being the gatekeeper for the many waves of guests who came to visit. In a twenty-four-hour period, I had suddenly become a caregiver, a friend, a trooper wife, a gatekeeper, a bodyguard, and so much more. It was overwhelming.

When the time came for me to leave the hospital after Bridget's mom arrived from out of state, I was frozen with fear. I sat in my car in the parking lot of the hospital crying, unable to move. I was going home to my parents to get my son, and my husband was staying behind to work. How could I just leave and go back to normal? How could I let my husband leave my sight? What if he calls me? What if another trooper calls me and delivers terrible news? Questions were running through my head. I called my father, who encouraged me and prayed with me and told me that I needed to push through and come home. He gently reminded me that my husband's fate is in our Father's hands and that if something is going to happen, it will happen whether I'm there in Midland or eight hours away. I again pushed thoughts down into a deep spot in my head and pushed through.

The weeks to follow were hard for me. I couldn't sleep when my husband was working the night shift. Every time I saw his name pop up on my phone, I half panicked and had to combat breathe before I answered the phone. I was constantly on edge, playing the "what if" game and waiting for the worst to happen.

I knew that I needed help, that I needed to talk to someone. I was encouraged by my parents to meet with

Dr. Tania Glenn, and I was incredibly nervous to go and speak with her. The day came and I am so thankful that she was able to help me through EMDR to be able to process all of the trauma of that day and the week after. She helped my brain properly file away all that happened during that period of my life. I am now able to process that day with more logic and less emotion. I can breathe again when my husband calls me. I am not panicking and constantly playing the "what if" game. Best of all, I am sleeping again! Getting help has provided me with the tools to be able to move forward with my life, to not be stuck in this rut of fear. Because of the healing process, I feel braver about facing the long career of law enforcement ahead of me and the task of being a law enforcement officer's wife.

Dana and Rob

Tara, Sawyer and Ryan

Rhanda and Kelly

Olivia, Mattea, Micah, and Isabella

Micah comforting Mattea when their dad had to go on patrol on Christmas Day

Payton

Erica, Henry, Son, Mari, and Hayden

Michelle and Chris

Michelle with Our Practice at the Annual 5K Honoring Chris

Chapter Four

Traumatic Events and Families

*In the heat of the moment
when fear has you frozen
You're crashing and burning
when life's at its coldest
Don't fall too far from who you are
Try to tear us apart
but know that we'll wear our scars*

"Scars" by I Prevail

Traumatic events are always sudden and unexpected. They seem to occur when families are cruising along in the rhythm of life, dealing with normal occurrences and life challenges, and then suddenly everything changes. Big events and traumas always seem to occur at the wrong time and under the worst circumstances, mostly because they magnify any issues a family might be dealing with at the time. Whether it's aging parents, a newborn baby, an unexpected employment change, or financial issues, traumatic events will magnify and exacerbate these issues. Life becomes a super challenge.

A trauma is a sudden, powerful, extreme event that

overwhelms the coping capacity of a first responder. Because first responders do not live in a vacuum, their families are impacted significantly as well.

The most important thing to understand about traumatic events is they are disruptive in every aspect of life. First responders and their families find that everything has changed—daily functioning, emotions, sleeping patterns, eating patterns, contact with friends and relatives, and sometimes even living situations. Nothing is off the table.

The Aftermath of a Trauma

Every public safety agency should have a plan for these types of events. In my book, *First Responder Resilience: Caring for Public Servants*, the first chapter is about having a plan in place and what a good plan looks like. Knowing that no two situations are the same, a good plan provides the guidance and checklists for a response with the flexibility for the current circumstances to be addressed.

The first issue many families face if their first responder is injured is dealing with the immediate crisis. Family members should be notified by the first responders themselves immediately if they are not incapacitated and able to make the call. Hearing their loved one's voice on the phone will significantly decrease the fear and anxiety of knowing that something bad has happened. Even a quick "Just so you hear it from me, I am okay" means the world to family members.

If a first responder is not able to make the call, family should be notified as quickly as possible. The circumstances of the situation will determine the best way to do this. If it is an injury, most loved ones want a phone call and definitely do not want the near heart attack they will experience if someone shows up at their door. Obviously in the worst-case scenario of a line-of-duty death, these notifications are always done in person (see Chapter Seven).

If a first responder is in the hospital, the next step is getting the family to them. Ideally this is done by someone in the department providing the transportation so that family members are not rushing to the emergency room and risking their own safety by being distracted and stressed.

At this point, it is very important for the department, the peer support team, and other family members to join in and help out. If a spouse or significant other comes from a large family, they may not need a lot of resources and help. If they are new to the area and have not connected socially to the community, they may need a lot of help.

Helping family members includes transportation, childcare, meals, assistance with hotel reservations, watching the first responder's home while no one is there, mowing the lawn, doing airport runs for family members who may be coming from out of town, and pet sitting, just to name a few.

I encourage peer support teams to sit down with the family and create a list of what they need, with as many details and contact numbers of family members as possible. I then ask peer support teams to create an account on a care- or helping-themed website and to populate as much of the services needed as possible on the website. Set with a relevant and easy-to-remember login and password, this information can then be sent to entire departments so the rest of the personnel and their family members can get involved and help out. This is by far the best way to get everyone on the same page, to organize a response, and keep a steady flow of help rather than overwhelming the family up front and then leaving them without help later on.

I highly encourage a very organized, clear response. I once opened the freezer at a law enforcement agent's house after a traumatic event and there were fourteen lasagnas in there. The family has been flooded with lasagnas in the first two days. Apparently, lasagna is the crisis food!

During this time, first responders should be able to meet with representatives from human resources to determine the type and length of leave they will need, along with any form of catastrophic or donated leave they might qualify for. It is very important that this is addressed quickly, so that a representative can communicate with the rest of the department should a need arise for donated sick leave.

As first responders are released to go home, the

assistance continues in the form of food, childcare, transportation, health care for injuries, and continued emotional support for the family members. This plan should continue on the helping website format and should be monitored to assure that the needs of the family are being met.

As a crisis calms down, many people forget that the family may still need assistance. After a helicopter crash in 2013, one of the peer support teams I work with had to carry the pilot upstairs once he got home due to his physical injuries. They did an amazing job creating the kinds of changes in the home so he could get around where he needed to until he healed. They also continued to assist during the four months of his recovery time. The crisis might have been over, but the needs were still very much there. This was a significant help to his wife, who was new to the area and really needed the kind of help the team provided.

Another immediate concern is the media. Oftentimes, first responders are named specifically in the news and are subjected to much public scrutiny. This is a very stressful time for everyone involved. Families sometimes need to vacate their home until the media frenzy passes. At a minimum, departments should implement a watch rotation over the first responders' homes whether they have vacated or not, just to assure the safety of everyone involved.

An additional tricky aspect of managing a crisis is social media. Unfortunately, in this social media world, loved ones often hear news via social media before they can be notified by their loved ones or the department. This is extremely traumatic and frightening for families. It creates panic and if a loved one is alone at home, it puts them right into crisis mode with no one around to help. Departments are encouraged to educate their personnel and family members regarding protocol after an event. While a department may not be able to control a spouse's social media usage, the education on how traumatic it can be to learn of an event on social media can help loved ones make informed decisions about social media usage when a trauma has taken place.

Another consideration is the social media accounts of first responders and their family members. Often after a major event, I recommend that first responders and their family members suspend their accounts for a while. This has become a significant avenue of personal attack on many first responders and their family members, and this will only serve to further the level of trauma the family is experiencing.

Finally, one of the biggest impacts of these events is on the children. Chapter Five describes the impact of a public safety career on children. During traumatic events, the best thing we can do for the children is to return them to as normal a routine as we can as quickly as possible. Children thrive on structure and safety. While it is impossible to return to complete normalcy in the immediate aftermath of a major incident, attending to the daily details of their normal routine will help children feel grounded and safe.

Special attention will need to be given to the school and the teachers, as outlined in Chapter Five. Parents need to be assured that the teacher is aware of the situation and closely monitoring what is being said both in the classroom and on the playground.

Middle and high school-aged kids must also return to as much routine as possible. Assuring them throughout these turbulent times and allowing them to express their concerns and feelings as much as they are willing to at this very difficult age is extremely important.

Recovering from a Trauma

Each person's response to trauma is very individualized. What we focus on in terms of first responders and family members and the ability to heal from trauma has much to do with two factors: individual interpretation and resilience.

We always start in understanding a person's trauma with their interpretation of the trauma, which is based on that person's history, prior experience, training to deal with high-stress situations, and their successful coping with past similar experiences. It is very common for people who go through the same event to have completely different interpretations of the event.

When someone indicates that they have "been there, done that" and state that a situation is not a big deal to them, their interpretation is likely based on their history. If someone from the same event says that this is the worst thing they have ever dealt with, again, it boils down to their interpretation based on their history. There is nothing wrong with either interpretation, and when we listen to a person's interpretation, their response to an event makes sense.

The key is to understand how people are interpreting an event and to provide the assistance they need at the time to get them through the aftermath. It is extremely important that no one responds callously or negligently to a first responder or a family member just because they might think that the situation is not a big deal.

The second factor, resilience, plays a big part in how people cope with the aftermath of a trauma. I see this all the time in my practice. First responders and family members with high resilience frequently bounce back quickly and easily while those with low resilience struggle to come back. In teaching resilience, we ask first responders to maintain high resilience because, as I like to explain, if we hand them the butt-kicking call of a lifetime and their resilience is high, they will heal faster. If their resilience is low, the healing is much more arduous.

Building resilience in first responder families starts simply. We focus on hydration, nutrition, rest, and exercise. Small changes in these areas pay off big. From there we build on resilience by focusing on the lives of first responders outside of the job. We work on family, faith (if this is a component of the first responder family's life), friends, and hobbies. Building resilience in a first responder family sometimes means going to marriage counseling, taking on the issues that need to be dealt with and strengthening the bonds within the family.

The key to resilience is to remember that no one is perfectly resilient. It is a work in progress our entire lives. It means that we are working, playing, loving, and living at the best level possible.

Getting Help

It is important to assure that families receive the help they need after trauma. As first responders heal, we want their families to heal as well. Resources should be in place for all family members should they need help.

In the immediate aftermath of a trauma, families respond very well to education, normalization, and the ability to discuss what has occurred. The model I developed for crisis intervention (outlined in *First Responder Resilience: Caring for Public Servants*) uses the acronym TEN FOUR. This stands for:

Triage
Educate
Normalize
Free discussion
Organize thoughts
Understand the big picture
Restore resilience

This model has been used not just for first responders, but for family members as well. Family members respond extremely well to this model and have given excellent feedback about how much it helped them understand what they were going through and restore a sense of normalcy.

After a traumatic event, the peer support team implements the "TEN" portion. They are responsible for triaging the entire situation for when they educate first responders and family members in appropriate settings and timeframes. Through the education of normal responses to trauma, they normalize what everyone is going through.

During the education briefs, first responders and family members engage in the "FOUR" portion. They can discuss their thoughts and reactions during this time of processing. It helps them organize their thoughts and understand the big picture. At this point, first responders and their family members can implement some methods to restore resilience and begin the recovery process.

The loved ones of first responders should get further help if things are not improving. Whether they see a therapist or use other methods for healing, focusing on rebuilding the mind and spirit is an important component of healing that frequently gets overlooked or ignored. Please remember that, as a loved one, it is okay to ask for help and important to heal.

Having a Plan

As stated before, every agency must have a plan. The plan outlines the steps to take, the resources needed, and the personnel who will be dedicated to each role or function in the plan. Having a plan also means having emergency funding to carry out the plan. Departments should begin to really assess the plans they have and to improve their plans if they are lacking. Hoping for the best is not a plan. Creating a good plan does not mean the worst will happen; it simply means you are prepared for it.

Each plan should absolutely take into consideration the needs of the family members. All too often, plans are made with zero mention of the family members. When these types of plans exist, all of the family's needs are somehow supposed to be met by the chaplain (if there is one) or the personnel closest to the impacted first responder. In these situations, agencies get what they pay for.

Poor plans lead to sloppy responses and years of bitterness from family members for the way they are treated in the aftermath of a trauma. This causes significant disruption for first responders both at home and at work. If a family member completely resents an agency for the way they were treated after an event, it's very difficult to ever get back to the way things felt and operated prior to the trauma.

A good plan addresses all of the potential needs in the aftermath of a trauma. This includes a budget for supplies, a peer support team, mental health clinicians who understand emergency services, and chaplains.

While a plan cannot dictate the roles or involvement of family members who come together to support a family in need, it is important to have a plan to work with these family members who want to assist. Incorporating them into the response rather than working separately or against these families is a great way to keep everyone moving in the same direction, to pace everyone, and to assure that no one is pushing themselves too hard.

All too often, those wanting to help get drawn into the process of assisting others and lose track of their own stress level awareness. It is very easy to get drawn into a situation and neglect your own needs because you are facing someone who needs so much more. Looking into the eyes of a distressed friend makes you forget your own stress. This is a very dangerous setup for vicarious trauma.

It is always extremely important in these situations that the peer support team leader sets the pace and the expectations for everyone and then follows through with making sure everyone is adhering to the plan. It is unacceptable to work sixteen-hour days while helping someone through trauma. I use the example of sixteen hours because I have seen it happen and it is absolutely destructive.

A good plan adheres to reasonable expectations, good pacing, and clean boundaries. I recommend that peer support, chaplains, and family members—whatever combination is available and best suited for the situation—always go in pairs. Two people should be responding to back each other up, to keep boundaries in check, and to pace each other. A crisis response day should be no more than six hours each day. Duties should be rotated so that all of the members of the response team are able to do both the more-intensive emotional type of work and the less-intensive logistical type of work. This is to prevent burnout and vicarious trauma.

How a Plan Comes Together

A recent event involving one of my customers is an excellent example of what a good response can look like. I would ask all leadership to examine if they are ready for a response such as this one. Fortunately for most agencies, a response does not require nearly the manpower, movement, and resources that this one did. I use this example to show an amazing type and level of response that can happen, given appropriate planning and budgeting.

A federal law enforcement agency was involved in a shooting in a remote location. During the course of the firefight, one agent was struck twice. Another agent stopped the threats. Two more agents were on scene, making a total of four agents involved in the incident.

The first priority was medical care, and the agency was able to remove the agents from the remote location and get all four of them to medical care. During this time, all agents were able to contact their spouses. Once the medical care was complete, all four agents were sent home. The agents' homes were in three different cities and two different states.

As soon as the firefight was over, a supervisor notified the peer support team. The coordinated response was implemented through conference calls and group texts, with peer support members responding from across the country.

Two members of the peer support team were sent to each agent's home within a day or two of their return, depending on the agent's preference. The team members met with the agents and their spouses. The first thing they did was to assess their situations to ensure that all of their physical and medical needs were being met. Then they educated couples on normal reactions to stress and how to restore resilience, and answered any questions they might have. This opened up much dialogue between the agents, their spouses, and the team members. The spouses all reported that the validation and normalization during these meetings were extremely helpful.

Due to the severity of the incident, we had already determined that my presence in each of the agents' homes was necessary. The peer support team did an excellent job explaining my role and putting the agents at ease about my visit. The team members assured them that my goal was all about prevention and mitigation of stress responses, and that my role was not to introduce any sort of challenges for their return to work.

I deployed to each of the four agents' homes and spent time with them and their spouses. At this point, I was able to clinically mitigate many stress reactions to the incident and give all four of the couples several ideas on stabilization techniques with their families. One spouse in particular was struggling significantly, so we addressed local resources, and she was able to follow through on finding ongoing resources that matched her needs.

Thankfully, all four families are intact, healing, and back on track in terms of their work and life balance. As it frequently happens, one of the agents was so pleased with the process that he has now put in his application for the peer support team.

Chapter Five

Public Safety and Children

*I just want you to see
What I've always believed
You are...
The miracle in me*

"Miracle" by Shinedown

There is no doubt that the children of public safety professionals grow up in very unique environments. Throughout my years of practice, I have noticed that public safety kids are some of the wisest, most resilient, and compassionate children there are. Being the son or daughter of someone who leads a life of service to others brings an awareness of life and humanity well beyond what most other children are aware of. It also brings its inherent challenges, which parents must be ready to deal with.

The Lifestyle

Just as spouses, partners, and significant others have to

adjust to shift work, to being on call, and to all of the scheduling nuances of public safety work, so do the kids. Not only are their parents gone for extended periods of time, kids in public safety families rarely experience the traditional holidays. They typically grow up with holiday celebrations not being on the actual holidays, and they adjust their lives and schedules just as much as their parents do.

Growing up in a public safety family also means that parents may miss games, tournaments, and birthdays. These children grow up with the flexibility and maturity of understanding that their parents have chosen careers with the obligations to protect others and save lives. They adopt this into their psyches at very young ages and tackle the events where parents cannot show up like the champions they are.

Once in a while, just like adults, the children of public safety parents will express frustration or dissatisfaction with the impact of the job on their lives. As children, they want their parents to be there for important events. This is normal. When this happens, it is extremely important for parents to hear their kids out and validate their feelings. It is also important to make special plans for when parents can be available. While this might not make up for the missed events, it does allow for special family events, traditions, and memories. These times are very important to the children, as we cannot expect them to sacrifice as much as the adults do. They did not choose this lifestyle and are frequently along for the bumpy ride without much say into the matter.

Many public safety families have adopted unique ways of managing schedules and the long absences of public safety members. These family traditions are recalled by the kids as one of their favorite things about growing up with first responder parents. With some creativity and flexibility, these traditions become some of the best parts about growing up in a first responder household.

Vicarious Trauma

Another unique aspect of being the child of a first responder is the very unique sense of realty they have. These kids grow up hearing stories, understanding adult choices and consequences, and sometimes hearing things they are too young to grasp. It is important for parents to monitor how much is said in front of their children. They may be too young to understand the details or to see the big picture. Overhearing stories they cannot comprehend can lead to anxiety about the work their parents do or about life in general. Having a good filter and sharing only what is age-appropriate with children is a very good way for first responder parents to minimize the chances their children will be vicariously traumatized.

In my career, I have responded to several air medical crashes. One in particular was very traumatic, as the crash involved four fatalities—three crew members and a pediatric patient. While I was helping the employees from this program, I met a flight medic who needed guidance about his three-year-old. He explained to me that he and his wife did not discuss the crash in front of their son, but that his son had been drawing pictures of crashed helicopters since the day of the crash. He even produced a picture his son had drawn, and it was clearly a helicopter that had crashed.

I explained to the flight medic that while he and his wife had not discussed the crash in front of his son, his child had most likely overheard the news, the talks he and his wife were having in private, and perhaps some of the dialogue between other crew members that had occurred at the post-incident gatherings. I went on to explain that kids are also very intuitive and pick up on emotions and energy way better than adults do.

We agreed that he and his wife needed to sit down with their son and answer his questions while explaining things in age-appropriate terms. I also recommended that he focus part of the discussion on safety and what flight crews do to prevent crashes so that his son could understand that these events don't happen randomly. Finally, we agreed that if his son continued to struggle, he would make an appointment with a qualified child therapist.

Another source of vicarious trauma is the media. Since the war on law enforcement began, we have experienced a sharp increase in the number of children of public safety members that we see at the practice. All forms of media and social media may be too overwhelming and confusing for young children. The exposure to misinformation, violence, and negativity is toxic for children. The most important thing parents can do is to closely monitor and screen what their children are exposed to.

In the aftermath of a trauma, parents must do everything they can to protect their children. In my book, *Protected But Scared*, I tell the story of the young son of a police officer who is confused by the news and the war on law enforcement. The book is a tool for parents and children to read together. It also suggests ways for parents and departments to approach and deal with the anxiety their kids are experiencing. From seeking counseling to having family days at the departments, it is important to validate feelings, allay fears, and provide avenues for the children to express themselves.

Traumatic Events

High-impact events—such as an officer-involved shooting, a failed rescue, or the accidental wounding or killing of a citizen—are significant and overwhelming, often for the entire family. When it comes to the children, they are certainly not immune to the stressors surrounding the situation. Just as we care for the first responders and their spouses or partners, we must also care for the children.

The first thing to consider is explaining to children at an age-appropriate level what has occurred. While trauma therapists are capable of doing this, we usually default to the parents to take the lead on this, and we can help the parents with any wording or guidance they might request.

Because children do not comprehend the world the way adults do and because they are impacted in very different ways based on their developmental stages, one of the best things we can do is return our children to a sense of normalcy as quickly as possible. Their schedule, what they eat, their activities, the ability to play, their school, and their friends are the constants that bring them comfort in a time of upheaval. While we may not be able to return to 100 percent normalcy right away, continuing as much structure and routine as possible is one of the best ways to keep children calm and feeling safe.

Under extremely difficult circumstances involving high publicity and the media, it may be necessary to have children stay with other family members or close friends. The media camped out in front of a house or fear of retaliation when a public safety professional's name is released are the key reasons to do this. These circumstances are very confusing and frightening for children, and safety becomes paramount.

Another consideration for parents is the school situation. After high-publicity incidents, I always recommend that the parents visit with their child's teacher and the principal to clarify what has occurred and set expectations for how the teacher needs to monitor the children and whether or not the teacher needs to address it with their class.

The idea is to prevent a traumatic scenario where a classmate of a first responder's child says or repeats something they heard at home, such as, "I heard your dad shot a teenager" or "I hear that your mom let a kid die" while they are unmonitored on the playground. This can and will cause incredible trauma, angst, and confusion for the child of a first responder. Suddenly school is no longer a safe place to be, and if this type of problem is not dealt with immediately and effectively, it makes school a daily dose of high stress.

When the children of first responders see a therapist, parents should first interview the therapist to ask and understand what their experience level is with the children of emergency services personnel. They should also ascertain their experience in working with trauma. Parents should also ask the therapist about their knowledge of the type of work the first responder does and the lifestyle of first responder families. If there are any hesitations, the parents should move on and continue to interview therapists until they find a comfortable fit for their child. I cannot stress the importance of this. A few years ago, I was brought into a situation where an uneducated therapist called the state child welfare system on the son of a law enforcement officer simply because the child acknowledged knowing there were guns in the house and where they were stored. This was completely unacceptable, ignorant, impulsive, and overall a really bad choice made by a therapist whose job was to help this child.

Two Amazing Interviews

I had the absolute joy of interviewing some amazing children of public safety professionals. What struck me is the sense of maturity and altruism these children already display in coping with the unique stressors of being first responder families. It is as if they realize they are already contributing to and serving their communities by living the lives of first responder families.

Isabella, Olivia, Micah, and Mattea

These four siblings are the children of a police sergeant. Isabella is sixteen, Olivia is fourteen, Micah is nine, and Mattea is eight years old. Their dad has been a police officer their entire lives.

Tania: What is different about having a dad who is a police officer?

Micah: It feels safer having a dad who is a police officer. Also, he leaves for a long time to work and he works long days.

Olivia: He came home one day and was making lunch and he got a callout and had to run out the door! He left the eggs on the stove.

Tania: What is it like when he's on night shift?

Isabella: We sometimes forget when he sleeps during the day, and we are loud. It's hard to keep up with.

Mattea: We are loud when he's not sleeping!!

Tania: What are the holidays like?

Micah: It's sad sometimes because he can't be home for dinner.

Mattea: He stops by to say hi, which is nice.

Tania: Is this tough on you?

Isabella: It's all we know. This is our normal.

Tania: What do you think about the work your dad does?

Micah: Awesome!

Isabella: It takes a lot of bravery, but the sacrifices are so much better than the bad. What we sacrifice is worth it to help others.

Tania: Do you have to remind yourselves of this?

Isabella: Yes.

Olivia: He broke his arm once. It made me realize how dangerous it is.

Micah: When he has to leave really fast, I get worried.

Tania: How do you know he's safe?

Olivia: Our mom tells us.

Micah: Sometimes if it's really late, we hear the sirens.

Tania: Who do you talk to when you worry?

Isabella: We talk to our mom and to each other.

Tania: What's it like with other kids at school?

Isabella: Our friends are super interested in our stories. They say their parents have boring jobs.

a first date and turned out to be the only date, I very carefully tempered my discussion about my work. I only mentioned what I considered funny stories or good outcomes from my emergency room world. His response was, "I really don't like your stories. They are awful." My internal dialogue included a simultaneous silent scream and the words, "And I'm out!"

While they can be an easy and natural fit, pure public safety couples do have their challenges. Between the impact of the work on their lives, the need to set boundaries with work, and the really tough times involving trauma, public safety couples frequently find themselves balancing the stressors of their work with being a loved one to a first responder. This is sometimes a very tricky balance.

The Impact of the Lifestyle

Shift work alone can be one of the most difficult aspects of public safety couples. Sometimes couples end up on opposite shifts and have very little time together. When children are small, public safety couples will frequently choose to be on opposite shifts to care for the children and eliminate the need for daycare. This is inherently stressful and tiring, and many first responder couples struggle during these times.

The focus for couples going through this should be quality versus quantity time. In other words, you might not have a lot of time together, but the key is to make the time you do have really count. Planning dates, fun activities, or even time to rest is essential for couples to do together.

It is also important for public safety couples to manage careers that may be competitive with each other. Couples who work for the same department have to balance the politics, the promotion process, and the setbacks that come with every career. Sometimes the roles at work can bleed over into the home, so recognizing, acknowledging, and problem-solving on ways to mitigate the impact that completing careers have on each other are extremely important priorities for couples to engage in.

Setting boundaries with work can also be a challenge for first responder couples. Talking about work is easy because there is usually so much to talk about! One of my pure public safety couples who came in for counselling quickly realized (with a nudge from me) that they spent a significant time talking about work and not much time on anything else. I challenged the couple to just talk about work for thirty minutes each day and the rest of the time to talk about other things. They came in the next week and admitted that this was extremely difficult! The husband said that for the first few days they stared at each other a lot when they couldn't think of things to talk about.

Another boundary that couples must set is how much they talk about their relationships at work. Disclosing too much information can be a very messy way to bring others into your relationship and puts a significant stressor on the home life. The couples who manage this the best are typically the ones who have already learned the hard way. The best rule of thumb for pure public safety couples at work is to speak of only the things about their loved one that are public or common knowledge. Items and details that one considers personal are for the home, as are marital struggles and challenges.

Trauma and the Pure Public Safety Couple

Traumatic events can have a very significant impact on first responder couples. All too often, when something happens, fellow first responders, departmental leadership, and even peer support teams make the mistake of assuming that the loved one of an impacted first responder is fine, or minimally impacted, because they understand or because they are on the job.

When a trauma occurs to a first responder, their loved one is dealing not only with the impact on their first responder, but also with their own impact, feelings, vicarious trauma, worries, and concerns. Because they are on the job, the loved one may be under significantly more pressure to maintain a façade of strength. If they worry about being judged for showing emotions, loved ones who are also first responders themselves will bury their emotions. This robs them of the ability and opportunity to heal.

When trauma happens, those in the position to assist must maintain a dual focus on the fact that a loved one is not only a first responder, they are also a significant other, spouse, partner, sibling, parent, etc. Whatever their relationship to the impacted first responder, they are a family member first and foremost. It is imperative to provide a safe environment that allows for the expression of whatever emotions they are experiencing and to assist them with getting the resources for healing.

The children of pure public safety couples can also be significantly impacted by trauma. If one parent goes through a traumatic event, the children may struggle with the fact that the other parent is still in the line of duty. Children are faced with managing not only the impact on them from the trauma, but also the fear of the other parent going through something similar. Depending on their developmental stage, it can be hard for children to express this verbally. Instead they may act out in ways that are not typical. Allowing children to attend play therapy with a qualified therapist who understands first responders may be a necessary step in a child's healing.

An important aspect of healing for children who have parents who are both in emergency services is the timing. When both parents are significantly impacted, many kids will lay low and manage through the crisis without much disruption. Then, as parents stabilize, the children will begin to act out. This is their way of telling the parents that the event frightened or confused them, and that it is time to acknowledge the event with the children and get help.

When trauma occurs in a family of first responders, everyone will need help at some point. While it is typical for first responders to go into the work mode of protecting and caring for their loved ones, eventually when the response mode slows down, it is important to give each person in the family the time, space, and tools they need in order to recover.

Henry and Erica

Henry and Erica are both deputies for a law enforcement agency located in Central Texas. While no relationship is perfect, these two exemplify the healthy balance a couple must maintain in order to both work in the field and simultaneously maintain a life outside the job.

Henry and Erica have both been through a significant amount of trauma. They reference these traumas lightly in the interview. To give their trauma context, here are more details regarding some of the events they have experienced:

While on a call for a significantly emotionally disturbed individual, Henry was kicked in the side of his head and neck at full force while attempting to restrain the individual in order to prevent this man from hurting himself. Henry was so severely injured, he had to be placed on light duty for a year while he recovered. The pain was horrible, the recovery process was arduous, and the financial toll on the family was almost devastating.

Henry still experiences head, neck, and back pain, and he deals with this on an almost daily basis.

During a time of severe flash flooding in Central Texas, a fellow female deputy was swept away by the floodwaters and was killed. No one could get to her calls for assistance fast enough to save her.

A sergeant who was a very well-known supervisor and who had a long career of exemplary service, staged his own suicide to look as though it was a homicide. After the funeral, the details of his life came to the surface. This was extremely difficult for many fellow law enforcement officers to understand and accept. At the time of the suicide, this sergeant was Henry's supervisor.

Most recently, Erica was driving home from work when she witnessed a person fall from a bridge over a highway she was on. Sadly, it was a driver for a package delivery company who was involved in an accident on the bridge, and because he did not have his seatbelt on and the side door was open, he was flung from the vehicle. Erica stopped and began lifesaving measures in hopes of making a difference. While she was performing CPR, she looked over and saw a picture of this man's wife and child in the back of the case on his phone. Suddenly everything Erica, Henry, and their children went through when Henry was injured hit her. Being the strong one was no longer an option. Erica began to struggle, but she didn't let it fester. She got help.

It has been such an honor to work with these resilient, spirited, energetic, and dedicated law enforcement officers. I hold both of them in such high regard.

Tania: How did you meet? Were you both already in law enforcement?

Erica: We met working in the jail.

Henry: Yes, we met in jail!

Erica: Henry was already heading to the street and I was brand new. Henry came to my pod delivering newspapers...

Henry: I did more than deliver newspapers.

Erica: He was behind this big guy, and I never saw him until he popped out from behind the big guy and I was like, "Where did you come from?"

Tania: Henry went to patrol and Erica—how soon did you go to patrol?

Erica: About a year later I was able to go to patrol, so we were both on the streets by 2012.

Henry: It was like going through the academy twice.

Erica: He didn't get to come to my graduation.

Henry: Nope—I was a new boot on the street, so my sergeant wouldn't let me go.

Tania: You went through all that and could not go to graduation? Doesn't that just say it all?

Tania: What are the pros of both being in public safety?

Erica: The fact that we can go home and talk about calls and totally decompress because we both get it. Some officers never get to tell their families because the families don't understand. For me, I don't have to explain anything. Also, when I was new, he was a field training officer so I could run stuff past him and that was really helpful.

Henry: For me, the fact that I don't have to worry about a meltdown is helpful. I am always extremely unlucky, and I am always where I don't need to be—yes, a black cloud—and when I get hurt, I don't have to explain why I was fighting someone.

Erica: We get excited about what we do— we look forward to doing ride outs with each other so we can see what the other person does. We are excited to be around each other and what we do.

Henry: I love watching her teach at the academy. I am proud of her.

Erica: It's cool being in work mode and seeing Henry do it.

Tania: What are the cons of both being on the job?

Henry: It's really easy to convey common anger to a problem. If I'm mad at the county, then she's mad at the county, so we both get mad.

Erica: I agree because I like to fight, and there are days when I want to fight with people for fucking with my husband.

Erica: When our work partners say stuff about Henry, it bothers me.

Tania: How do you keep people in your agency out of your relationship?

Erica: People leave us alone for the most part. They know better. They don't mess with us, but we are respected as a couple.

Henry: They joke with me that whatever fight or pursuit I am in is the easy part because going home is the hard part! I returned from being injured and a lady tried to stab me in the face. I joked that it wasn't the first time a lady tried to stab me in the face!

Erica: It helps our marriage that we play around all the time. We talk shit and wrestle a lot. We have always been like that.

Henry: We are who we are!

Erica: Another con is that since he was injured, I worry more. He has struggled to heal. He was home almost a year. It was really hard to not worry. I don't think I dealt with it until recently. Since the injury, I worry a lot more.

Erica: I do feel better that he has a K9 now. But I can't live in fear, and I am finding the balance between worry and knowing he will be okay.

Tania: Let's talk about the impact of trauma on you guys. There have been some tough times in your agency. What have you learned through managing them?

Erica: When I first went to the street, I had an incident and I personalized it. The agency was good to me. Henry was really great for me too—he was there. Then we lost a sergeant and things were really bad. We both struggled and that's how we met you. Then Henry was injured, and we had to keep going. We have a family, and we have kids to provide for. We have figured out the balance between talking to each other and talking to others. Therapy has been so helpful for both of us. Henry always looks so different after therapy, and I am so glad we found this outlet.

Henry: The first thing that got to me was when a deputy drowned. No one said anything. No one talked about it. The day of her funeral we worked and never talked about it. We just kept going. Then we lost the sergeant. That one was different. No one talked about it again, and I needed to talk about it. That's what pushed me over the edge. I started having issues and couldn't sleep. Everything was shitty. I was referred to you and I got to deal with it for the first time. Then I came to see you immediately after I got hurt because I knew I needed it.

Tania: Is it safe to say that if something happened tomorrow you two would communicate openly with each other and come back to therapy?

Erica and Henry: Definitely!

Tania: Tell me about your kids. What is their life like having police officer parents?

Erica: Our oldest boy, we call him "Son," and our daughter Mari have been through a lot because of their biological father. It brought us together to support them. Son worries about us, and he was impacted when Henry got hurt. They like to listen to our stories. Mari rides out with Henry and she loves it! We try to talk to them about our jobs, and we are open with them. Hayden is five, and he thinks it's cool. He says he wants to be a cop. Sometimes he says he wants to be a fireman so we tell him no!

That's not acceptable! Our kids are strongly based in reality.

Henry: They acknowledge and roll with what we do. It's great. We have great kids. Hayden started therapy when I did—I used to bring him all the time!

Tania: He was so good! He would sit there and occasionally say, "Daddy, I am ready to go," and then he would just wait while we talked. So cute!

Tania: Is there anything you want to say to other pure public safety couples?

Henry: Don't talk to other people at the agency about your spouse. Don't bitch to your coworkers. You can't do that—it will destroy your relationship.

Erica: I would say just to support each other. Be each other's biggest support. Talk, vent, be open-minded, and know how to read them. Encourage them to get help when they need it.

Henry: Don't try to be a cop when you are listening to them. Just listen to know how they are doing with things.

Chapter Seven
The Unthinkable

*Call your name every day when I feel so helpless
I've fallen down but I'll rise above this,
rise above this*

"Rise" by Seether

This chapter addresses line-of-duty deaths. It is difficult to read. It's okay to put it down and pick it back up later, or to read it when you are at a point where you can get through it. This chapter is about the worst-case scenario. It's hard for me to write it, but it's so important because should the absolute worst event happen, we all need to be ready.

While most departments have protocols for line-of-duty deaths, from notifications to the funeral, I aim to address the details that often get overlooked or are done incorrectly. I also want to address the recovery process. I finish this chapter with an amazing testimonial from an amazing woman who brings so much hope to others.

The Immediate Aftermath

What I explain to first responders and family members after a line-of-duty death is the fact that everyone is going through traumatic grief. When you combine a trauma with grief, you are handed the awful, gut-punch experience of traumatic grief. It is complicated, it hurts like hell, and it takes time and effort to heal from traumatic grief.

After a notification occurs, it is a time of total chaos for the family members. The first and most important thing to remember when assisting family members after a line-of-duty death is to start at the base of Maslow's Hierarchy of Needs—food, water, clothing, shelter, and safety are the main needs we have during and immediately after a crisis, and everyone goes to these needs immediately after a trauma.

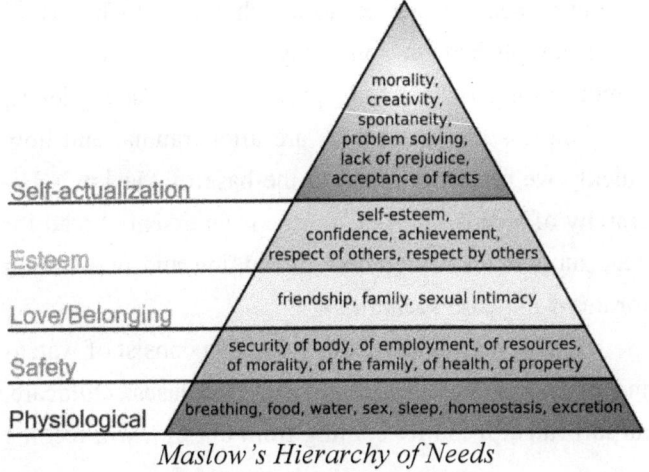

Maslow's Hierarchy of Needs

I encourage departments, peer support teams, other family members, unions, support groups—everyone involved—to meet up and get on the same page. Establishing an account on a care-provider website is the fastest, easiest way to get everyone organized and on the same page. It prevents the fourteen lasagnas from arriving on day one, and it prevents the failure to provide necessary assistance on day forty-one. My favorite site is www.lotsahelpinghands.com. Pacing everyone through the ever-changing needs of the family on the receiving end of services is the most effective way to assure that these needs are being met. The account should be updated periodically based on progression through the trauma, and eventually discontinued when the family is ready.

In her book *Crazy Courage*, Samantha Gallagher-Light shares the journey of the immediate aftermath through her recovery after her husband was killed in the line of duty. She speaks of how her friends had to pull her out of bed and get her to the shower, which was all she accomplished on some days. What Samantha was demonstrating is how truly profound traumatic grief is, how helpless the loved ones are after trauma, and how quickly we all get dropped to the base of Maslow's Hierarchy of Needs. *Crazy Courage* is an essential read for peer support team members in training and preparation for the worst-case scenario.

The level of care at this point can consist of watching over a home, meals, grocery purchases, childcare, airport runs for family coming from out of town, feeding the pets, mowing the lawn, and cleaning the house, just to name a few. A loved one facing traumatic grief will be oblivious to all the needs that have to be met during this time.

I also encourage helping the family make decisions about finances at this point. I once witnessed a widow in a total haze of grief and despair mindlessly open her mail, which was full of donations from across the country. There are so many good people and organizations who send thousands of dollars to family members after line-of-duty deaths. This widow had a stack of mail with checks totaling tens of thousands of dollars, but she didn't care. She just wanted her husband back. Realizing this was her mortgage, her kids' tuition, and her financial stability, we were able to contact her CPA, who made recommendations on how to manage this money to her advantage and who was also able to help us carefully secure this money for her.

During this turbulent time, it is imperative that those in line to assist family members maintain a clear, consistent, steady schedule with clearly defined roles and boundaries. This is how I train my peer support teams for these types of activations because I have seen things turn drastically wrong.

Specifically, I mandate that my team members work no more than eight hours a day during activations because the events are mentally and physically draining. I ask them to be ready for me to tell them to stand down, go to the gym, or go home when I notice they are fatiguing or overwhelmed by the intensity of the situation. I do not allow them to work twelve- or sixteen-hour days, because I firmly believe this causes damage to those helping out. The last thing I want is for peer support team members, who are extremely valuable assets, to experience burnout and quit the team.

Additionally, when team members go to the family members' homes, they always go in pairs, and the pairs rotate out every few hours. Many times, I have witnessed one peer support or department team member designated as the family point of contact. They will spend hours with the family, are exposed to significant traumatic grief responses and emotions, get very little sleep, skip their workouts, skip meals, ignore their own families and, at the end of this, are a complete train wreck. They are exhausted, burned out, raw, and out of patience. Their own family is angry and resentful. Put this combination of two very raw people under one roof, and it is the argument of a lifetime. No one is happy, and no one knows what to do about it. This is completely unacceptable.

Another reason those responding need to go in pairs is to prevent trauma bonds. While trauma pulls us together and bonds us in a way that feels very deep and meaningful, a trauma bond is just that—it's a bond based on a trauma. A trauma bond is developed through the feelings of empathy and closeness that result after going through an experience together. It feels exhilarating and sometimes exciting. It is extremely easy to get drawn into a trauma bond. The danger here is that it's a set-up for lines to get crossed and for boundaries to become fuzzy.

Simply put, the danger of one person being assigned to a family is if this person comes from the agency where the first responder worked, they wear the same uniform, do the same job, make the same money, etc. They soon represent replacement husband, wife, mother, or father. It's a very subconscious pull. It does not start out as intentional. But it happens. It destroys families even more. I have seen it happen, and there is absolutely no reason to create a scenario where this becomes a risk.

The Long-Term Aftermath

As agencies get through funerals and families attempt to establish some sense of normalcy again, departments and peer support teams should continue to provide the necessary support. As we heal, human beings begin to move up Maslow's Hierarchy of Needs to the emotional healing and human connections we need to have. This is when family members need emotional assistance.

At this point, the support must continue. Keeping up with the care website, notifying department members of what is needed next, can keep everyone involved consistently. It may be in the form of transportation to therapy appointments, memorials, dedications, and other types of events that honor fallen first responders. This must be a time of absolute diligence and focus for departments. A sudden cessation of support will only traumatize the family all over again. Being left alone suddenly to pick up the pieces while everyone else goes on with life is unacceptable. The level and types of support may slow down, but special care and consideration must occur so it does not come to a complete stop.

It is very important for family members to get emotional help after a line-of-duty death. Counseling, retreats, camps, massages, and self-care are all ways to begin the healing process. Reaching out to others and connecting with people who have been through similar experiences can be very helpful. Knowing you are not alone and having a team of people you can call on your worst days is a lifesaver.

As families move on, I firmly request that agencies and peer support teams allow for this. Whether they move away or stay in the community, remain single or get remarried, everyone seems to be full of opinions about this, but it is really no one's business. I once heard a group of first responders comment about a widow dating again, a year after her husband died. I return-fired my comment, which was something along the lines of, "Really? You are going to judge her for dating again? Do you go home to an empty house every night and feel the pain of losing someone you loved more than anyone in the world?" That seemed to make an impression because the judging stopped. What families do or don't do after they lose a first responder is for no one to judge or comment on. It is theirs to figure out.

I can't think of a better way to finish this chapter and this book than with Michelle's story. My team and I absolutely adore Michelle. She is featured in the documentary we produced because she is brilliant. Michelle is a remarkable woman who gives so much hope to others based on her resilience, tenacity, and courage. Personally, every time I see Michelle, I choke back tears, even after all this time. Part of the reason is because it brings back memories of such a terrible time for the tiny Hutto police department, but mostly it's because I am so proud and in awe of her.

Michelle's Story

June 24, 2015 started out like any other day. What would I change if I knew this day was about to change my life forever? I have asked myself this question many times. The details of this day have been written and rewritten in my head, as if I have control to change the past.

Let me start over by introducing myself first. My name is Michele Kelley. I am the widow of fallen officer Chris Kelley. Chris and I had a typical law enforcement family life. Our children were born into this life, as their dad had already become a police officer before they were born. Although they would miss their dad at birthday parties, on Christmas morning, and at Easter Services, they always knew Chris' job was important; therefore, the entire family made sacrifices, and I would do what I could to fill in the gaps for them.

Being a police wife was not for the faint of heart. I had to be the disciplinarian and nurturer on many nights. I had to learn to be okay with just the kids and me as we went places and people would always ask where Chris was. I had to learn that there would be a change of schedule almost anytime we would try to schedule lunch while he was on duty, as a call seemed to always come through. As a police wife, you must find a way to adapt to the abnormal schedule while also having faith that your officer will come home safe.

I worried about Chris at times, but I felt confident in him and his skills. I had to learn that adding anxiety to the unknowns would not help my children or me, so I leaned into my faith and the confidence I had in my husband and the police officer he was. Chris was in law enforcement since enlisting in the military in 1995. He then became a civilian police officer in 2006, when he settled in at the Hutto Police Department. In 2014, Chris became the detective sergeant for the Criminal Investigations Unit. During this time, our family finally got to experience a somewhat normal schedule, when we saw him many nights, weekends, and holidays. It was a change that we were blessed to have.

Going to that tragic day on June 24, 2015. It was a typical Wednesday morning. Chris and I were both getting ready for work. Each day before Chris would leave, the kids and I would give him a kiss, tell him we loved him, and for him to be safe.

Later that morning while I was at work, a friend

sent me a text asking me if I knew what was going on in Hutto, as there were many first responders with their lights and sirens on. I told her I didn't have any idea but I would ask Chris. I texted Chris a few times. Each time I received no response. I started to become panicked, so in my third and final text, I pleaded with Chris to text me back, for him to just tell me he was okay. I never received a text back.

A few minutes later my boss came to get me, as I was in a meeting. I did not think that him asking to speak with me had anything to do with my husband. I walked with my boss to his office. As I entered his office first, I remember turning back around toward the door to find the chief of police standing in the doorway. In that moment I did not know how, but I just knew Chris had died from the look on the chief's face. I remember falling to my knees. I remember the sounds around me were silent, as if I could not hear. I remember being able to look at my life as if it was in slow motion. I remember everything and nothing all at the same time. This is what happens when your body goes through trauma, I am told.

To have to call your family is something you will never forget. Every word of it. No one wants to be that person but I HAD to be that person. My life before was not the same. Our dreams were no longer. What WE had was no longer. I couldn't take that thought and just knew I had to go see Chris in the hospital. Although these moments were incredibly hard, they were also incredibly healing. This was something I needed. I had to see the man I called my husband. The man behind the badge. The father to my children. I had to hold his hand one last time. I had to tell him I loved him one last time. I had to kiss him one last time.

At the hospital, there was a lady named Christi with Victim Services. She came with me to my home as I asked her how I was going to tell my children. This was scary and so heart-wrenching to even think about. My children were four and seven when their dad died. They had gone on a field trip that day, and when they came home, my daughter thought we must be having a party since there were so many cars at home. She came running in, telling me she passed her swim test, and she had the best day ever! In that moment I began to sob as I knew I had to break her heart in a way it should never be broken. As a mom, you protect your kids from getting their hearts broken, so to have to be the one to do it— this will stay with me forever. My daughter began to scream as I told her that her daddy had died. She screamed, "Are you telling me I don't have a daddy anymore?" In that moment, my life and their lives were shattered.

If it weren't for Christi, for my family, my friends, the chief of police and his family, my neighbors, and the local police departments, I would not have been able to take a step forward from that moment. These people were angels in my life. They helped my children by taking them for fun outings, as I would stay home and cry. They helped by bringing food to feed us. They helped by listening and supporting us. They changed my lightbulbs and cut my grass. They helped get me to appointments. In these moments, asking for help wasn't an option. It was a necessity.

An entire community came together behind my family as they lit up blue lights and placed blue ribbons everywhere. Fundraisers were graciously given for us. So much love from people we had never met. Chris was the first officer to be killed in the line of duty in our town, so this was heartbreaking for so many.

How can a family heal from such a terrible tragedy? I chose to start by having my children and me go to counseling. My children did play therapy to work through their trauma and emotions, and I worked with a different counselor to work on my own trauma, emotions, and now raising children alone. This helped us a lot. We didn't always have the words, so counseling helped give us a voice. We also attended groups and camps for widows and children of fallen officers. They helped us to not feel alone. After the first year we attended camp, my children came home saying all the kids were just like them. You see, no matter how many times adults told them there were other children who had lost a parent, they couldn't see it with their own eyes, and therefore they felt alone.

As the months went on, although I felt counseling was helping, I still had images in my head that haunted me every day. When I went to bed at night, as I would drive down the road, even as I took a shower. I found out about EMDR and decided to give it a try. Tania Glenn was my therapist. From the moment I walked into her office to the time I left, I felt lighter. I felt different. I wasn't quite sure how one session could make me feel better and kept waiting for the images to come back. Years later and they still aren't back. EMDR unlocked so much trauma for me. For some it is smells or for others it could be the actual event itself. For me it was the images I saw over and over. For me it was my husband lying in his coffin. This image haunted me because, to me, it didn't look like him. Due to the severity of the injuries, it made it difficult for me to look at him lying there.

After experiencing this weight being lifted, I spoke with my children's therapist and thankfully she was also trained in EMDR. After much talk, my daughter and I decided she should try it. The part that my daughter struggled with was that now each time she would see a group of cars at our house or at someone else's house, she immediately would think someone had died. She would get anxious and worried because of the day when she came home and there were a lot of cars. EMDR did amazing things for her too. She was able to work through so many traumas once EMDR was completed.

I cannot understand how something so seemingly simple can be so life-changing, but it is. Whatever the trauma is, the first step is to reach out! Please do not think you can do this yourself. You are not alone unless you choose to be. We are almost five years out now, and

Micah: They always ask if he has shot anyone. I always say, "No, just a dog."

Tania: Are there any kids at your school who are afraid of police officers?

Simultaneous: No!

Tania: Anything else you want to share?

Isabella: We can't have friends inside when dad is sleeping.

Olivia: My parents are very overprotective of us and our lives. Because of what our dad has seen, we don't have certain social media apps. And he tells us not to steal CK underwear!

Tania: Is your dad super wise to things kids do?

Simultaneous: Yes!

Tania: Is he stricter?

Simultaneous: Yes!

Tania: Does he tell you some of the things that go on so you understand his worries?

Olivia: He does and that helps.

Micah: We like to hear the stories.

Mattea: People get angry and they scratch the road—it's weird. That was a call he ran: a woman was literally scratching the road with her fingernails.

Tania: Does that make you thankful for your home and safety?

Simultaneous: Yes!

Isabella: One weird thing that happens is people knock on our door because he has a take-home car, and they yell about a fight going on at their house, or they bring us stray dogs—because he is a police officer! We have had dogs in the backyard before that weren't ours!

Micah: This lady would knock on the door instead of calling 911. Luckily, she moved.

Tania: Do you watch the news?

Isabella: Not really.

Micah: They put bad things about him on the news. They said he hurt a woman who was drunk and fell.

Tania: Did that bother you?

Micah: I was sad because they were lying.

Tania: Did you talk to your parents about it?

Isabella: Yes. And we did not watch the news coverage. For a while he had to leave his car at the station too.

Micah: And on Halloween we weren't going to hand out candy so we had to take Dad's car to the station because he didn't want people to vandalize his car while we were gone.

Tania: I have noticed that the children of police officers have to carve out little things in life like this. You guys handle this like champions!

Tania: Is there anything else?

Micah: Sometimes I pray that he doesn't get hurt.

Payton

Payton is ten years old. Her father is a firefighter and her mother is a 911 call taker and telecommunications spe-

I can say the biggest impact for us has been counseling, EMDR, camps, and our support network! Life will never be the same for us. There will never be a day that we do not miss Chris.

Where there is darkness, there is light. This is the motto I have told my children. We use this motto to live, to fully live. I wanted them to know it's okay to be sad and to cry, while it is also okay to have joy and laughter. It is okay for us to live, as Chris would want nothing more than to know we can be happy again. Joy is something you can choose to have. We choose JOY!

In closing…

May 13, 2014, Washington DC: I am there for National Police Week to assist many families in honoring their fallen officers. This is an amazing week in so many ways, but also very draining and emotional. The sound of bagpipes triggers my tears every time. I have heard bagpipes all week.

I was stressed. Because of what I do, I know way too much. I remember wondering, "Why can't I just have a normal job?" The response that came to me was perfect. "This is your normal. It's what you do and who you are. If you did anything else, you would be bored."

Over the next six months, I bought a house, moved, had knee surgery, had a post-operative scare, responded to some major incidents and a whole host of other events that typify life. Life goes forward.

I have reflected on these words over and over, especially during rough moments. This is our normal, and it is what we do. And now, when our normal is too overwhelming, when it's too traumatic—when life is pushing us down—we lean on each other, we ask for help, and we pull together as a community. Because we are family.

About the Author

Tania was three months from completing her Master's Degree at the University of Texas when she witnessed the dramatic and violent standoff between law enforcement and the Branch Davidian Cult in Waco, Texas. At that point, she knew her calling was to work with first responders and to focus on healing these warriors from the horrors of post-traumatic stress disorder.

Tania spent the first ten years of her career working in a Level II Trauma Emergency Department on weekend nights as she built her private practice during the week. In 2002, Tania transitioned to her private practice on a full-time basis and has dedicated her entire career to working with first responders and military members.

Tania assisted with the aftermath of the Oklahoma City Murrah Federal Building bombing, the 9/11 attacks on the World Trade Center, Hurricane Katrina, the Dallas Police shootings, and numerous other incidents. Tania is referred to as the "warrior healer" by her colleagues, and she is passionate about her work.

Tania resides in Central Texas. Her loves include her family, her pets, and fitness.

Tania has three other books published by Progressive Rising Phoenix Press:
First Responder Resilience: Caring for Public Servants
Protected But Scared
Code Four: Surviving and Thriving in Public Safety

Progressive Rising Phoenix Press is an independent publisher. We offer wholesale pricing and multiple binding options with no minimum purchases for schools, libraries, book clubs, and retail vendors. We offer substantial discounts on bulk orders and discounts on individual sales through our online store. Please visit our website at:
www.ProgressiveRisingPhoenix.com

If you enjoyed reading this book, please review it on Amazon, B & N, or Goodreads. Thank you in advance!

www.ingramcontent.com/pod-product-compliance
Lightning Source LLC
LaVergne TN
LVHW040618250326
834688LV00035B/624

cialist. Both of her parents have been first responders her entire life.

Tania: What is it like being the daughter of a dispatcher and a firefighter?

Payton: If I ever get hurt, they know what to do or how to do it! And my mom really knows how to communicate with me when I need to talk to her.

Tania: Do you feel like you can talk to them about anything?

Payton: Oh yes!

Tania: Do you think you can talk to them about anything because they are used to dealing with difficult situations?

Payton: Definitely.

Tania: What are the holidays like?

Payton: They are pretty good. We don't fight. They do work holidays sometimes so we have a babysitter who takes care of us.

Payton: When my nana passed away, it was tough on all of us. She died at our home, and my dad knew what to do because he is a firefighter and he sees this stuff.

Tania: What's it like when dad works twenty-four-hour shifts?

Payton: I get to see him sometimes, and we talk on the phone when he is on duty. He works sometimes for two shifts in row and that feels like a long time.

Tania: Do you ever worry about their safety?

Payton: Yes, sometimes. I worry especially when

First Responder Families: Caring for the Hidden Heroes

dad goes into fires. I don't like that.

Tania: What do you do when you worry about your dad?

Payton: I usually distract myself with my phone. I don't worry as much as I used to, though.

Tania: What do other kids think about what your parents do?

Payton: My friends don't really say anything about what they do. Their parents have normal jobs.

Tania: Are you proud of your parents?

Payton: Yes!

Tania: What's it like with your mom working nights?

Payton: She kisses me goodbye, and we text when she is gone.

Tania: Do you watch the news?

Payton: No, it makes me nervous.

Tania: Do you feel like your parents are more strict than other parents?

Payton: They are when it comes to safety.

Tania: Do your parents tell you stories from work?

Payton: Dad tells Mom stories from work, and I eavesdrop.

Tania: When you eavesdrop, do you hear cool stories?

Payton: Sometimes and sometimes not. Sometimes they are scary. He usually only talks about problems at work.

Tania: Is there any story in particular that you remember?

Payton: There was this one person who ran a 5K and didn't drink water, and she went home and was like ugh!

Tania: Is there anything else you want to tell me about being the child of first responders?

Payton: I feel like Mom knows more than other parents might know about how to deal with problems. It definitely has its qualities. Sometimes it's bad because they are gone a lot.

Chapter Six

Pure Public Safety Couples

You've got something real here
You've got something real here
You've got something real here
I want you to know

"Got Something Real Here" by Paul Di Leo

It is no accident that first responders end up together. Given the shiftwork, lifestyle, stressors, challenges, and unique qualities of this type of work, many first responders learn quickly that it is a comfortable and safe fit to be with someone who understands easily and completely why you do what you do.

I recall my short-lived attempt to date "normal people" during my mid-twenties, when I was working weekend nights in a Level II trauma ER and building my practice (dedicated to first responders) on the weekdays. Besides the absolute impossible nature of dating someone who worked Monday through Friday during the day, there was the challenge with just making things fit. On the last date with a "normal person," which was actually